THE **MINI** ROUGH GUIDE TO
HELSINKI

T0016562

ROUGH
GUIDES

YOUR TAILOR-MADE TRIP
STARTS HERE

Tailor-made trips and unique adventures crafted by local experts

HOW ROUGHGUIDES.COM/TRIPS WORKS

STEP 1
Pick your dream destination, tell us what you want and submit an enquiry.

STEP 2
Fill in a short form to tell your local expert about your dream trip and preferences.

STEP 3
Our local expert will craft your tailor-made itinerary. You'll be able to tweak and refine it until you're completely satisfied.

STEP 4
Book online with ease, pack your bags and enjoy the trip! Our local expert will be on hand 24/7 while you're on the road.

PLAN AND BOOK YOUR TRIP AT
ROUGHGUIDES.COM/TRIPS

HOW TO DOWNLOAD
YOUR FREE EBOOK

1. Visit **www.roughguides.com/ free-ebook** or scan the **QR code** opposite

2. Enter the code **helsinki674**

3. Follow the simple step-by-step instructions

For troubleshooting contact: mail@roughguides.com

10 THINGS NOT TO MISS

A PERFECT DAY

9.00am

Helsinki Cathedral. After feasting on a Finnish breakfast at your hotel, head straight for the Neoclassical Kruununhaka district. In the morning light, before the crowds descend, the startling white cathedral floats above Senate Square like a dream.

10.00am

Havis Amanda. Wander down Unioninkatu to have a gander at the city's sauciest mermaid. Next, stop at the orange tents on the Market Square for a fortifying slug of coffee before admiring the many stalls, tumbling with fresh produce.

11.00am

Archipelago tour. Helsinki is a city of the sea. The Royal Line boat tour threads between the archipelago islands, offering stunning views of Suomenlinna Fortress and a whole new perspective on the city.

1.00pm

Lunch in Esplanadi Park. Back on dry land, head for lunch at the 140-year-old Restaurant Kappeli (see page 112), in prime position on tree-lined Eteläesplanadi. A favourite of Sibelius's, the restaurant has one of the biggest terraces in the city, perfect for people-watching and listening to live music on the nearby summer stage.

2.00pm

Walk up Mannerheimintie. Stroll through the park to the beginning of Mannerheimintie. This is Helsinki's longest street: on the left-hand side are venerable institutions such as the Parliament Building and the National Museum; while on the right are the modern Kiasma and Musikkitalo.

IN **HELSINKI**

Stop at Finlandia Hall to admire the work of Alvar Aalto, one of Finland's greatest architects, before taking a pleasant walk across Hesperia Park to the Olympic Stadium.

4.00pm

Olympic Stadium Tower. Although the Olympics were held here over sixty years ago, walking into the stadium will still give you goosebumps. However, the highlight of a visit is a clanking lift ride up the tower for fabulous views of Helsinki and its archipelago backdrop.

5.00pm

Sauna. Catch tram number eight (Arabia direction) along Helsinginkatu and prepare yourself for a quintessentially Finnish experience. Kotiharjun, dating back to 1928, is a rustic wood-burning sauna where you can get to know the locals. Pace yourself with plenty of breaks and cold water and remember your flip-flops as the floors are hot.

6.30pm

Sámi Dining. The metro from Sörnäinen will whisk you back to the centre in ten minutes, hopefully with an appetite. Lappi Ravintola (see page 115), a cosy wooden affair on Annankatu, can supply a taste of the wild north, with dishes of reindeer, wild mushroom, and Lappish cheese served with cloudberry jam.

8.00pm

Live music. Helsinki's operas and orchestras take a well-deserved rest over summer, but the city is full of music. Tavastia is a popular rock bar with a fantastic atmosphere and Storyville offers live music every night in summer.

CONTENTS

OVERVIEW

If you're looking for riotous razzmatazz, a sleepless, strung-out, 24-hour city where the party never ends, look elsewhere. Helsinki is a city of cool northern charms, floating serenely above the hot-headed European mainland. One of the world's newest capitals, it is a city that rewards the curious. If you want something unusual – fascinating architecture and design, offbeat galleries and museums, a piquant blending of east and west – you've come to the right place.

Helsinki is one of the world's most liveable cities, a safe, tolerant, modern metropolis with a clear identity of its own. Startling new buildings are transforming the city's silhouette, but its dwellers are still people of the forests and lakes at heart, with a passion for nature that is reflected in Helsinki's many gorgeous parks and gardens.

CITY OF THE SEA

Long referred to as the "Daughter of the Baltic", Helsinki owes its fortune to the sea. The city was founded to compete with the Hanseatic port of Tallinn, just across the Gulf of Finland, and the great offshore fortress Suomenlinna was built two hundred years later to protect this vital harbour. In post-war years, shipbuilding was a major industry, and Helsinki is still a centre for specialised Arctic ships, with sixty percent of the world's icebreakers being built in its western dockyards. Today, however, cruise ships have taken over from the merchant vessels and battleships, bringing in over four hundred thousand visitors each summer.

The sea and Helsinki are intrinsically linked. Salty inlets poke their way into metropolitan boulevards, and countless yachts and ferries thread their way through the archipelago islands. The city has even captured a piece of the Baltic and built a kind of shrine around its edges. Public edifices such as Musikkitalo Music Centre, the Winter

Gardens, the modern library, Linnanmäki amusement park, and two stand-out Alvar Aalto buildings, the Opera House and Finlandia Hall, encircle Töölönlahti Bay, the peaceful watery core of the city's cultural and recreational area. The entire Katajanokka district, stuffed with Art Nouveau buildings, appears to be tethered to the mainland, floating alongside it like a boat. Fishermen still sail their catches into the harbour, mooring beside the bustling Market Square to sell their wares. And as if Helsinki doesn't have enough saltwater, there's a new lido underneath the spinning shadow of the SkyWheel.

Only during the long, cold winter does the water finally rest. Even the Baltic freezes into an endless expanse on which promenaders can walk dogs or try out their cross-country skis. At the weekend, city-dwellers strap on their skates and take an icy spin around the inlying islands of the archipelago, masters of the frozen waves.

MEET THE FINNS

In Helsinki, the vast majority of the people around you are Finnish-speaking while there is a small percentage of Swedish-speakers. Notwithstanding the overwhelming dominance of Finnish, the city's street signs are more often than not shown in both languages – with Swedish beneath the Finnish.

Whatever their language, the Finns, by and large, are quiet people and to outsiders may seem rather

Café life

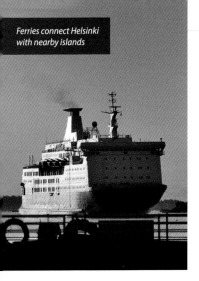
Ferries connect Helsinki with nearby islands

introspective, though easy to talk to as seventy percent speak English. As the old joke goes, you can recognise an extroverted Finn because, while conversing, he looks at your shoes rather than his own. But make an overture and you'll receive real kindness and curiosity in return: unlike a London or a Rome, with their hard-faced, hurrying millions, Helsinki is small and relaxed, with time to consider its visitors.

Finns are patriotic – their blue-and-white national flag is on display everywhere – and are rightly proud of their country's natural beauty. A great deal of importance is placed on spending time in the whispering forests of spruce and birch. In high summer, Helsinki empties as its inhabitants head for that quintessentially Finnish retreat, a rustic *mökki* (summer cabin) on the shores of a glassy lake.

Escaping into nature is vital to the Finnish soul. Helsinki's many offshore islands are popular beach and bathing places in summer, and there are two national parks on its doorstep where city-dwellers go to fish in fine weather, or to pick berries and mushrooms as autumn draws in.

Conversely, Finns also have a rampant addiction to technology – perhaps not so surprising, since Finland is where Nokia phones were pioneered, developed and revolutionised. The City of Helsinki has opened up data to its citizens, so that everyone can participate in improving its public services, and much of the centre is covered by its free Wi-Fi network.

ARCHITECTURAL HERITAGE

Helsinki was founded in 1550, and only evolved into a large city in the late nineteenth century. Consequently, it has not grown up from higgledy-piggledy medieval roots like most other European cities but had an orderly plan from the start. After it was made Finland's capital in 1812, Helsinki benefited from the astonishing talents of German architect Carl Ludwig Engel, who poured his creativity into Senate Square and its surroundings. Helsinki was the World Design Capital in 2012, with €16 million being used to enhance the city with projects including the construction of the unusual Kamppi Chapel of Silence and the Kulttuurisauna public sauna.

Helsinki also has big dreams for the future: its run-down industrial areas and former docklands are in the process of being rejuvenated. The old abattoir quarter is now a centre for food; Suvilahti power plant makes a dramatic venue for open-air music festivals; and Kalasatama harbour is being transformed into a visionary residential area, with eco-designed high rises and floating apartments, that will become home for twenty thousand people by 2030.

CLASSICAL MUSIC

This country of just over 5.5 million has also produced a disproportionate number of conductors and classical performers. The importance that Helsinki gives to its musicians is reflected in the prominence of buildings such as Finlandia Hall, Musikkitalo and the Opera House, which sit in stately splendour alongside the Parliament and National Museum. Finnish composer Jean Sibelius (1865–1957) is celebrated in frequent concerts. 2015 marked the 150th anniversary of his birth, which was celebrated in Helsinki with a packed programme of special events.

HISTORY AND CULTURE

Finland is one of Europe's newer countries: it celebrated its one hundredth birthday in 2017. However, this vast, sprawling territory has been the stamping ground of many different peoples across the centuries. The first definitive evidence of human settlement shows that Sámi people had moved into the region by around 8300 BC. The Sámi were gradually displaced into the far north by incoming Fenno-Ugrian tribes, who migrated from the Ural Mountains and the Volga River plains, located to the southeast in present-day Russia. By 2000–1000 BC, forms of Finnish were spoken on both sides of the Gulf of Finland.

The early settlers were subsistence hunters and fishermen, but by around 500 BC, agriculture had become the dominant way of life. Stable settlements grew up first along Finland's coast, spreading inland by the middle of the Finnish Iron Age. Around AD 800–1050, Vikings occupied what is now the southern coastline of Finland as a trade route to the east.

A sixteenth-century map of the Nordic countries and Lapland

THE SWEDISH ERA

During the early medieval period, the area now known as Finland was coveted by both its western and eastern neighbours – the Roman Catholic Swedes and the Greek Orthodox Novgorod Republic (Russia). Sweden mounted three Crusades against Russia, with the territory of Karelia being the juicy fought-over bone. The Third Crusade, in 1293, split Karelia between east and west, establishing the Catholic–Orthodox border that was to stand for many centuries. Vyborg/Viipuri, with its imposing castle, was founded to defend the line.

Swedish political and social systems flourished, but Finnish peasants retained their personal freedom and were never serfs. Finns were given the right to vote in the election for the king in 1362 and later for representation in the Swedish Diet (parliament). From the late fourteenth to the early sixteenth century Denmark, Norway and Sweden were united in the Kalmar Union. The Lutheran Reformation reached Finland in 1527, initiating a surge of interest in the Finnish language. The prominent proponent of the Reformation, Mikael Agricola (1510–57), Bishop of Turku and creator of written Finnish, translated the New Testament into that language in 1548.

THE FOUNDING OF HELSINKI

Helsinki, or Helsingfors in Swedish, was founded by King Gustav Vasa of Sweden to offer trading competition to Tallinn, the Hanseatic League city on the opposite side of the Gulf of Finland. To achieve this, he issued an edict on June 12, 1550, ordering citizens from Rauma, Ulvila, Tammisaari and Porvoo to move into the new town at the mouth of the River Vantaa. This date is now celebrated as Helsinki Day. At that time the town was very small and became even smaller when many of its inhabitants were killed by plague and a great fire that struck in 1570. Growth was slow, but continuing wars saw Helsinki become an important military centre and a winter haven for the navy. By 1640 the town had moved to its present location, further south on the Vironniemi headland. In 1654 another great fire caused devastation, only to be followed

Ode to the brave

Finland's national poet, Johan Ludvig Runeberg (1804–77), wrote the epic poem *The Tales of Ensign Stål*, which commemorates the bravery of the Finns during the disastrous 1808–09 war. The first section of the poem was later adopted as Finland's national anthem, *Vårt land (Our Land)*.

in 1710 by a further outbreak of plague that killed approximately 1200 people – around two-thirds of the population.

In 1700 the Great Northern War broke out between Sweden and Russia, and in 1703, Russia, a growing power, built a new capital at nearby St Petersburg. During what was known as the 'Great Hate', from 1713–21, Russia occupied Helsinki. The Russians were driven out, returned two decades later; and after this, Sweden's position as a superpower began to wane. The Swedes reinforced Helsinki against the Russian threat by beginning construction, in 1748, of the sea-fortress of Sveaborg – now Suomenlinna – on a series of small islands guarding the marine approaches to the city (see page 61). When completed some forty years later, it was considered the 'Gibraltar of the North'.

This brought increased prosperity to Helsinki, and seafaring trade developed significantly, but more trouble was on the horizon. Fires destroyed Helsinki in 1808 and, in the same year, political machinations between Napoleon and Tsar Alexander I forced Sweden into the disastrous decision of declaring war on Russia. In the Peace Treaty signed the following year, the Swedes accepted that they had lost control of Finland. The country was then annexed to Russia as an Autonomous Grand Duchy in 1809.

RUSSIAN RULE

Finland's new ruler, the Russian Emperor Alexander I (1809–25), proved lenient. Finland was given an extensive amount of autonomy and was able to retain both its Lutheran religion and Swedish as the official language. In 1812, Helsinki replaced Turku as the capital of the Grand Duchy of Finland. In 1827 Finland's only university burned down in the Great Fire of Turku; when it reopened the following year, it did so in Helsinki.

Helsinki flourished under Russian rule, with the new capital rebuilt in monumental Empire style by Carl Ludwig Engel and Johan Albrecht Ehrenström. During this period the city's population increased to around fifty thousand– four decades earlier it had been just four thousand– and daily life was very similar to that in other European cities. Kaivopuisto and Hanko Spas were extremely popular with the affluent classes, who were not allowed, by law, to travel outside the empire to seek such pleasures elsewhere.

The Battle of Poltava ended Swedish domination

This period of peace and prosperity ended with the Crimean War (1853–56), which was fought on many fronts. Sveaborg (Suomenlinna), the gateway to St Petersburg, was bombarded by twenty thousand shells during a period of 46 hours but remained standing.

FINNISH VERSUS SWEDISH

During the reign of Alexander II (1855–81) sections of the population began agitating for the Finnish language to be a joint official language with Swedish, an end achieved in 1866. After more than fifty years of absence, the Finnish Diet met in 1863, and fifteen years later the Conscription Act raised a Finnish army.

Helsinki became Finland's administrative centre, and the opening of railway lines – to Hämeenlinna in 1862 and St Petersburg in 1870 – ensured that it also became the industrial heart of the country. Coinciding with this industrialisation, grand neo-Renaissance buildings – most notably along Esplanadi, Aleksanterinkatu, Mannerheimintie and Erottaja – began gracing the city. Finally, after a period of more than three hundred years, Helsinki achieved the primary ambition of King Gustav Vasa of Sweden, and eclipsed Tallinn as the most important city on the Gulf of Finland.

As Russian nationalism flourished during the reign of Alexander III (1881–94), and even more so during that of Nicolas II (1894–1917), its adherents grew impatient with the privileges enjoyed by the autonomous Grand Duchy of Finland. Russification, the policy of overturning Finnish separatism, flourished in Russia, although

THE FATHER OF FINLAND

Carl Gustaf Emil Mannerheim (1867–1951) is one of Finland's greatest heroes, a warrior who pitted his country's meagre forces against the might of Russia in three bitter wars. He was perhaps an unlikely figurehead: Mannerheim served in the Russian Imperial Army for thirty years. However, following the October Revolution, his allegiance was all to Finland.

Mannerheim's most memorable leadership came during the Winter War of 1939–40. Appointed Commander-in-Chief of the Finnish forces, he oversaw a guerrilla offensive against Russia that lasted a brutal 105 days. The Red Army had vastly superior numbers, but the Finns were fast, adaptable and equipped to deal with temperatures that fell as low as –43°C. Russian casualties were almost five times higher than those of the Finns, causing great embarrassment to the Russian regime.

After World War II, Mannerheim became president of Finland, guiding the country from war to peace. Such was his prestige that his funeral, on a bitter winter day in 1951, brought Helsinki to a standstill. The Mannerheim Museum (see page 56) is a fascinating memorial to the Father of Finland.

Finland itself was undergoing radical reform. The old Swedish Diet was replaced by a unicameral parliament in 1906, with MPs voted for by universal suffrage. Finland was the first country in Europe, and second in the world (after New Zealand), to allow women to vote and to stand as MPs, and its first parliamentary session had a total of nineteen women representatives.

INDEPENDENCE

The new century saw the construction in Helsinki of grand new buildings like the Central Railway Station, the National Museum and Kallio Church, all in Art Nouveau (*Jugendstil*) style. The first Finnish opera was performed in 1852, and this became an established national art form. Jean Sibelius (1865–1957), composer of nationalistic works such as the *Karelia Suite* (1893) and *Finlandia* (1899), was awarded a lifetime state grant in 1897 so that he could concentrate on composition.

As Russia underwent the October Revolution, Finland seized the opportunity to declare independence on December 6, 1917, and Helsinki became the capital of the Sovereign Republic of Finland. Yet the continued presence of Russian troops within the new country's boundaries caused turmoil that resulted in a bloody civil war. A coalition of Finnish Socialists and the Russian Red Guard was pitted against the White Army (led by General Carl Gustav Emil Mannerheim), backed by the Imperial German Army. Following the Russian defeat, Finland's independence was assured. After flirting with the idea of becoming a monarchy,

International settlers

Over the last ten years, the number of foreigners living in Helsinki has more than doubled. Today, foreign-language residents make up fourteen percent of Helsinki's population, with the largest groups coming from Russia, Estonia and Somalia.

Finland adopted a republican constitution in 1919.

Shortly afterwards a new style of architecture surfaced, most notably in the impressive silhouette of the parliament building, which opened in 1931, and the stadium built for the 1940 Olympic Games (postponed until 1952 by the outbreak of war).

On November 30, 1939, more than a million troops from the Soviet Union attacked Finland. The Finns, heavily outnumbered, repulsed the attacks and inflicted heavy losses on the Russians, but were forced to cede the southeastern part of the country to the USSR.

Mannerheim

During the so-called Continuation War (1941–44) Helsinki was attacked by much heavier air raids but suffered comparatively little damage, and Finland became the only country in continental Europe involved in World War II not to be occupied by foreign forces.

THE YEARS OF DANGER

During the period 1944–48, known as the Years of Danger, a communist takeover was still considered a possibility. This threat was averted by the Treaty of Friendship, Co-operation and Mutual Assistance (known as YYA in Finland) with the Soviet Union in 1948. This guaranteed Finland's sovereignty but committed the country to defend its borders against Germany, or any state aligned with Germany, that could use Finland to attack the Soviet Union.

Alvar Aalto's Finlandia Hall

The post-war years saw Finland struggling to pay off immense war reparations to the USSR, amounting to US$300 million. The government invested heavily in the metal and shipbuilding industries, and Finland changed rapidly from a mainly agrarian to a modern industrial country. The debt was finally paid in 1952, after which the country began to look outwards once more. Finland joined the United Nations in 1955 and became a full member of the European Union on January 1, 1995. With its growing confidence, a new, more modern, style of architecture emerged, epitomised by the work of Alvar Aalto: examples in Helsinki include Finlandia Hall (1971) and the Opera House (1993).

MODERN HELSINKI

Today, Helsinki has a population of almost 665,000, a figure which is expected to increase by 35,000 by the year 2030. To deal with this, there are ambitious and innovative projects to transform the former harbour/industrial areas of Jätkäsaari and Kalasatama into new commercial and residential areas, and to extend the metro system to outlying districts. The centre too is changing: new homes are being built along the western side of the railway lines, and there are ambitious plans for the Töölönlahti Bay area (see page 45), though unfortunately the Covid pandemic slowed the pace somewhat.

IMPORTANT DATES

c. 10,000 BC First inhabitants arrive in Finland as the glaciers retreat.

500 BC-AD 1300 Finnish Iron Age.

1155-1293 Three Swedish Crusades against Russia.

1527 Lutheran Reformation reaches Sweden.

12 June 1550 King Gustav Vasa of Sweden founds Helsinki.

1713–21 and 1742 Russia occupies Helsinki, marking Sweden's decline as a superpower.

1748 Construction of Suomenlinna fortress begins.

1808-09 Sweden declares war on Russia and is defeated; Finland annexed to Russia as an Autonomous Grand Duchy.

1812 Helsinki becomes the capital city, rebuilt in monumental Empire style.

1866 Finnish made the joint official language with Swedish.

1906 Finland introduces universal suffrage, becoming the first European country to grant women the vote.

6 December 1917 Finland takes advantage of the Russian October Revolution to declare independence: a short civil war follows.

1919 Finland adopts a republican constitution.

30 November 1939 The Soviet Union attacks but is repulsed by Finland's vastly inferior number of troops.

Post-war years Finland evolves from an agrarian country to an industrial one.

1952 Helsinki hosts the XV Olympic Games, postponed from 1940 by WWII.

1955 Finland becomes a member of the United Nations.

1970s onwards Alvar Aalto initiates a modern style of architecture.

1 January 1995 Finland joins the European Union.

2002 The euro replaces the Finnish mark.

2015 The city celebrates the 150th anniversary of Sibelius's birth.

6 December 2017 Finland celebrates one hundred years of independence.

2020 The Covid-19 pandemic causes travel bans and a two-month long lockdown in Finland.

2021 The new Covid-19 vaccine sees widespread uptake in Finland, with the highest number of vaccinated people recorded in Helsinki and Uusimaa.

2023 Finland joins NATO after the Russian invasion of Ukraine.

Tram passing by an
Art Nouveau building

OUT AND ABOUT

Helsinki is on an oddly shaped peninsula, nibbled at by the Gulf of Finland, which convolutes itself into numerous inlets, bays and harbours around the edges of the city. Initially, this can be a little disorientating; but you'll soon find your way around. This is a small capital, and most of its attractions are centrally located. Before striking out independently, it can be worthwhile taking the **Panorama Sightseeing Bus Tour** (see page 125), which gives a good overview of the city's main sights with a recorded commentary in multiple languages.

Visitors arriving by train or airport bus will be deposited at the Central Railway Station, at the very core of the city. The station sits in the northwest corner of a rectangular area between Mannerheimintie to the west, the Esplanadi in the south, and the Senate Square and Market Hall to the southeast. It is within this rectangle that the majority of Helsinki's hotels, shops, bars and nightclubs are to be found.

Cruise ships dock at one of four harbours: South Harbour, Katajanokka (both around 1.5km/1 mile southeast of the station), West Harbour and Hernesaari (both around 3.5km/2.2 miles southwest of the station). All are linked to the centre by frequent trams or buses.

Most places of interest can be reached comfortably on foot, but if you are footsore or short of time, there's a good public transport network. This includes a metro (subway) system, although most visitors prefer to remain above ground and use the tram or bus systems, which all converge at Central Railway Station.

It's hardly worth hiring a car, even if you're exploring further afield. There are frequent train services to Tampere and Turku, both just under two hours away; and Porvoo can be reached by a short

Wikström's solemn figures adorn Helsinki Railway Station

bus ride. Tallinn, in Estonia, on the south side of the Bay of Finland, is linked to Helsinki by high-speed ferry.

RAUTATIENTORI

The **Central Railway Station** ❶ (Päärautatieasema) is Finland's most-visited building: more than four hundred thousand people pass through it each day. Designed by Eliel Saarinen and inaugurated in 1919, it links two of Helsinki's most prevalent architectural styles, National Romanticism and Functionalism. The monumental structure certainly makes a strong first impression on visitors: sheer pink-granite walls make ants of the hurrying crowds, and the massive, four-sided clock tower is a prominent landmark. The station's front doors are guarded by four muscular giants, the *Lyktbärarna*, each holding a translucent lantern. These solemn figures, designed by Emil

Wikström, were taken down for a bath in 2013 – a complicated task when even a single head weighs 1.5 tonnes. Commuter and long-distance trains, including trains to Russia, leave from the Central Railway Stations, and the central Metro station lies below it.

Railway Station Square (Rautatientori), to the east of the building, serves as an open-air bus station and has, on its north side, the National-Romantic-style Finnish National Theatre, which has been the theatrical company's home since 1902. An oversized statue of playwright and novelist Alexis Kivi (1834–72) stands outside. He is now recognised as one of Finland's greatest writers, although he died in obscurity.

WINTER IN HELSINKI

The nights may be long and the weather bitter, but so what! As the Finns say, "Life gets no better by pulling a face"; and there are plenty of attractions to stave off the winter darkness.

The twinkling fairy lights of St. Thomas Christmas Market fill Senate Square for most of December; the night sky explodes with fireworks on New Year's Eve; and in early January, the Lux Helsinki light festival makes the city glow – literally.

And of course, this is the time for seasonal ice-and-snow fun. The whole of the Railway Square is transformed into an open-air ice-skating rink, Jääpuisto Ice Park (Dec–Mar, check website for latest information; https://jaapuisto.fi/en), while Keskuspuisto (Central Park), just north of the Olympic Stadium, contains several trails which are suitable for cross-country skiing.

When the skies are cold and clear, you can also see the Northern Lights from Helsinki – pick a dark corner of the city and watch for the pulsing, flickering light show.

ATENEUM ART MUSEUM

On the south side of Rautatientori, at Kaivokatu 2, is the Neoclassical façade of the **Ateneum Art Museum, The National Gallery of Finland ❷** (Ateneumin Taidemuseo, Suomen Kansallisgalleria; tel: 0294 500 401; Tue–Fri 10am–8.30pm, Sat–Sun 10am–5pm; charge; www.ateneum.fi). Inaugurated in 1887, it represented a huge investment for a small country, and its collection of more than twenty thousand works of art is the largest in Finland. The works of Finnish artists date from the 1750s to the early 1960s (works from 1960 onwards are on display at the Kiasma, Museum of Contemporary Art, see page 40). Much-loved national treasures include Akseli Gallen-Kallela's *Boy with a Crow* (1884) and two pieces inspired by Finnish mythology, *Lemminkäinen's Mother* (1897) and the *Aino Myth* triptych (1891); Hugo Simbert's enigmatic *The Garden of Death* (1896) and *The Wounded Angel* (1903); and several beautiful works by Albert Edelfelt depicting scenes of rural Finnish life. There's also a small selection of international art (Van Gogh, Gauguin, Cézanne and Chagall).

Stockmann's department store ❸ (see page 95) a Helsinki institution, takes up an entire city block at the junction with Mannerheimintie and famous for its window displays. The stand-out

The National Gallery of Finland is housed in the nineteenth-century Ateneum

sculpture here is the **Three Smiths statue** (1932) by Felix Nylund, depicting three naked blacksmiths hammering on an anvil. If you look carefully around the base, you can still see damage caused by bomb shrapnel, inflicted during the 1944 Continuation War.

THE ESPLANADI

The elegant semicircular façade of the **Swedish Theatre** (Svenska Teatern),

Sausage building

The Ateneum's neighbour is the *Makkaratalo* (Sausage House), which gained its nickname from the sausage-shaped band encircling the third floor of its raw-concrete exterior. Voted the ugliest building in Helsinki, it is nevertheless protected by the National Board of Antiquities as an example of 1960s Brutalist city planning.

dating from 1866, dominates the western end of the **Esplanadi ❹**, Helsinki's most emblematic park. Two streets – Pohjoisesplanadi (North Esplanade) and Eteläesplanadi (South Esplanade) – run either side of the long, narrow strip of greenery, all the way down to Market Square. Pohjoisesplanadi is home to small shops, bars and restaurants, including the ever-popular Café Esplanad, the Kämp Hotel, and the summer-only tourist office (No. 19), while Eteläesplanadi has larger institutions. These two elegant neo-Renaissance rows replaced older wooden buildings in the second half of the nineteenth century.

The bronze figure in the middle of the park is J. L. Runeberg (1804–77), the national poet who wrote the lyrics for the Finnish national anthem. Two other statues of eminent men at the western end commemorate the writer Zacharias Topelius (1818–98), and the poet Eino Leino (1878–1926). At the eastern end of the park is the city's most famous statue, ***Havis Amanda*** ❺. Erected in 1908, the fountain features a naked mermaid intended to

Stalls in the he Old Market Hall

represent Helsinki rising from the sea. It was unveiled amid great controversy, but today is one of most widely admired symbols of the city. At 6pm on Walpurgis Night (April 30th), students gather to wash the statue and place a tasselled cap on her head, marking the start of the carnivalesque May Day celebrations.

MARKET AND SENATE SQUARES

The bustling **Market Square** ❻ (Kauppatori) is one of Helsinki's real delights. Its year-round market (Mon–Fri 6.30am–6pm, Sat 6.30am–4pm, summer Sun 10am–5pm) bursts with colourful produce and souvenirs in summer, and you can buy fresh fish directly from small boats moored at the quayside. If you're peckish, there's also a motley collection of outdoor cafés housed in tents. The square is the venue for the lively Baltic Herring

Market, a week-long seafood festival held each October. It quietens down during winter but is still worth a visit. The granite **obelisk** topped by a two-headed eagle was Helsinki's first public memorial, erected in 1835 to commemorate Empress Alexandra's visit to the city two years before. The eagle was removed by Russian sailors during the Revolution but flew back to its golden perch in 1971.

Along Eteläranta, the now renovated red-, white- and yellow-brick **Old Market Hall** ❼ (Mon–Sat 8am–6pm, Sun 10am–5pm; http://vanhakauppahalli.fi) offers a fascinating array of stalls selling delicatessen-style foods, including bear meat, bakery products and all kinds of other goodies.

Massive Tallink Silja ferries dock in the **South Harbour** opposite. In winter, the frozen sea can reach a thickness of 50cm (20in) – an impressive fleet of icebreakers keeps the channels clear. Ferry boats to Suomenlinna (see page 61) depart from this harbour. Between May and September, you can also catch a boat here for an archipelago cruise. Three companies offer 30 min-3hr Helsinki sightseeing trips: **IHA-Lines** (tel: 09 6874 5050; www.ihalines.fi), **Strömma Finland** (tel: 09 2288 1600; www.stromma.fi) and **Royal Line** (tel: 0207 118 333; www.royalline.fi). The latter also have cruises to destinations a little further afield, such as river cruising in Porvoo or island hopping in Espoo.

Across the street from the Market Square, the long, low building with the bluish-grey façade is the **City Hall** (Pohjoisesplanadi 11–13), dating from 1896, with the city's coat-of-arms depicted on the tympanum. The stately white building on the corner is the **Presidential Palace**, constructed in 1820 by a merchant with grand ideas. Seventeen years later, it was purchased by the Russian Tsar to serve as his local palace when visiting Finland. After Finland gained independence, the building became the official residence of the president. The building is still used for important presidential receptions, but these days the man himself lives in a more modern house near Seurasaari.

On cobbled Sofiankatu, **Helsinki City Museum** ❽ (Helsingin kaupunginmuseo; tel: 09 3103 6630; Mon–Fri 11am–7pm, Sat–Sun 11am–5pm; free; www.helsinginkaupunginmuseo.fi) has frequently changing exhibitions that always unveil some interesting aspect of Helsinki's history.

KATAJANOKKA DISTRICT

Katajanokka, a boomerang-shaped island jutting from the eastern side of the city, is connected to the centre by two short bridges where locals like to cast their fishing rods. The district contains a ferry port and a quiet, well-to-do residential area, whose elegant streets make for pleasant wandering. Unfortunately, the first thing you see crossing the Kanavakatu Bridge on to Katajanokka is one of Alvar Aalto's least successful efforts: the dirty white marble Enso Gutzeit Office Building (the "sugar cube"), dated 1962.

Helsinki Allas (tel. 04 0565 6582; Mon–Fri 6.30am–9pm, Sat 8am–10pm, Sun 9am-9pm; charge; http://allasseapool.fi) is an exciting harbourside development located between the Market Square and the beginning of Katajanokka. It consists of a spa, saunas, two full-length

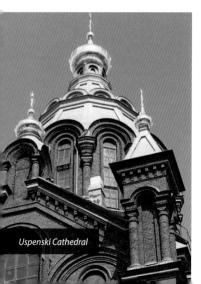
Uspenski Cathedral

sea-water swimming pools, a children's pool and a diving pool. On the quayside next to the site, the 40-metre (130ft-) high **FINNAIR SkyWheel** (tel. 040 480 4604; Mon–Thurs 10am–9pm, Fri 10am–10pm, Sat 10am–10pm, Sun 10am–8pm, hours change outside of summer months; charge; www.skywheel.fi) takes you on a twelve minute revolution, with views of the Market Square and the city's two cathedrals.

Uspenski Cathedral ❾ (Tue–Fri 10am–4pm, Sat 10am–3pm, Sun noon–3pm; closed Orthodox feast days; free), consecrated in 1868, is the district's most captivating sight. This brick behemoth is the largest Orthodox cathedral in the Western world, built to make a statement after the Russians defeated the Swedes in 1809. Its green copper roof is studded with thirteen small golden cupolas, representing Christ and the Apostles – it's actually more impressive from the inside, where four immense painted granite columns support the star-studded dome. Glittering chandeliers and a gilded iconostasis add to the air of opulence.

A further 100m/yards from the cathedral is **Luotsikatu** ❿, Helsinki's best-preserved street of Art Nouveau (*Jugendstil*) houses. Many of the buildings on this and nearby streets were designed by the architectural team of Gesellius, Lindgren and Saarinen, and all abound with unusual details. Don't miss the beautiful carved door at No. 1 or the sad-looking little creatures above the entrance at No. 5.

Other interesting structures on the island include the icebreakers moored on the northern side; the long, yellow nineteenth-century naval barracks (Merikasarmi), designed by Engel, which now house the Finnish Foreign Ministry; Helsinki's former county prison (Helsingin lääninvankila), transformed in 2007 into a rather unusual hotel; and the *Jugendstil* Customs and Bonded Warehouse (1900), beside the Viking Line terminal, with its grey turrets and round red-brick towers.

Cathedral and statue of
Alexander II on Senate Square

SENATE SQUARE

The historical **Kruununhaka** district contains many fine nine-teenth-century buildings. After Sweden's defeat in 1809, Helsinki became the capital city of the newly created Grand Duchy of Finland. Tsar Alexander I naturally wanted a capital worthy of the name. He chose Johan Albrecht Ehrenström, a military engineer, to sweep away the cramped medieval streets and put something splendid in their place. In Ehrenström's vision, **Senate Square** ⓫ (Senaatintori) would become the symbolic heart of the new Grand Duchy, with all the main institutions placed around it according to a strict hierarchy of function. The Prussian architect Carl Ludvig Engel (1778–1840) was chosen to design and oversee the whole project, a job that took him a quarter of a century and resulted in some thirty dazzling Neoclassical buildings.

Today the square is a national meeting place; huge, excited crowds gather for celebrations such as Independence Day,

December 6, and New Year's Eve. A statue of the "good Tsar" Alexander II watches over the festivities from the centre of the square. Dating from 1894, the statue is surrounded by images representing Law (*Lex*), Peace (*Pax*), Light (*Lux*) and Work (*Labour*). Stand at the Tsar's feet to best hear the sound installation **Senaatintorin Ääni**, a five-minute digital carillon composed by Harri Viitanen and Jyrki Alakuijala, which plays at 5.49pm every day.

HELSINKI CATHEDRAL

The shining white **Helsinki Cathedral** (Tuomiokirkko; tel: 09 2340 6120; Mon–Sat 9am–6pm, Sun 11am–6pm, until 9pm in summer; charge; http://helsingintuomiokirkko.fi/en) dominates Senate Square, its massive columned façade topped by a huge dome. The building is in the shape of a Greek cruciform and is sparsely decorated, inside and out. From the rooftop, 3m- (9.8ft-) tall statues of the Apostles gaze over the city, the largest collection of zinc sculptures in the world. The only focus points in the curving white interior are the gilded organ, pulpit and altarpiece, flanked by angels, and statues of the Reformation leaders Luther, Melanchton and Mikael Agricola.

Engel worked on the cathedral blueprints from 1818 until his death in 1840. Construction began during his lifetime, but it was not until February 15, 1852 that the building was consecrated. It was originally known as the Church of St Nicholas – after

Guard Parade

The Guard Parade has become a popular sight in the city. At 12.30pm on summer Fridays, the Finnish Defence Force band marches with much pomp and ceremony from Senate Square to Esplanadi Park, where an hour-long concert then takes place.

Aerial view of the Cathedral and Katajanokka

both the patron saint of trade and seafaring, and Tsar Nicholas I – and was upgraded to cathedral status in 1959.

The cathedral can seat a congregation of 1,300, and the vaulted crypt, which is only open in the summer, is used as a venue for exhibitions and concerts. Engel also designed the two chapels on either side of the two-tiered bank of steep steps; the one to the east is still used as a chapel, and the bells and a café are contained in the western one.

STATE BUILDINGS AND THE UNIVERSITY

The first building to be constructed on Senate Square was the eastern Imperial Senate (1822), which became known as the **Palace of the Council of State** after Finnish independence. Today it houses the prime minister's office, the office of the chancellor of justice, much of the ministry of finance, and the government's conference rooms – cabinet meetings are held here every Thursday at 1pm.

The columns and porticoes of the pastel-coloured building were designed to reflect the Roman Senate. The country's oldest public clock, the handiwork of master clockmaker Jaako Juhonpoika Könni, adorns the façade.

Turku Academy, the country's first university, was founded in Turku in 1640 but was destroyed by a devastating fire in 1828. Turku's sad loss was Helsinki's gain: the university was transferred to the young capital and given a prestigious location on the west side of the Senate Square. It was renamed the Tsar Alexander University and renamed again in 1919 to become the **University of Helsinki**.

Adjacent to the cathedral, the pale-yellow Empire-style **University Library** (tel: 02941 23920; Mon–Fri 9am–8pm, Sat 10am–4pm, varies out of term time; http://freewww.helsinki.fi/kirjasto) is one of the world's most beautiful library buildings and is considered Engel's masterpiece. Take a few minutes to admire the marvellously ornate Cupola Hall, designed to resemble Roman baths. The upper area is supported by 28 marble columns, their pinnacles gilded with gold leaf, with the images and ornaments on the domed ceiling symbolising knowledge and learning. Unfortunately, Engel didn't live long enough to witness the library's opening in 1840.

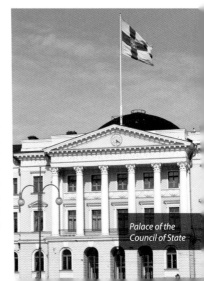

Palace of the Council of State

Behind the square, on Aleksanterinkatu 16–18, and recognisable by its blue façade and white columns, is **Sederholm House** (Sederholmin Talo; tel: 09 3103 6529), which dates from 1757 and is the oldest stone building in Helsinki. It belongs to the city council, and now houses the Helsinki City Museum (see page 32), a favourite with the little ones with its fun Children's Town.

MANNERHEIMINTIE

Mannerheimintie, Helsinki's busiest and longest street, was named after the respected Marshal of Finland in honour of his 75th birthday in 1942. Baron Carl Gustav Emil Mannerheim (1867–1951) was a political and military leader, explorer, general in the Russian Imperial Army and President of Finland from 1944–46, and perhaps

THE FOUR ESTATES

Before the present parliamentary system came into being, the country was governed by a Four-Estate Diet. The votes of three of the four Estates (Nobility, Clergy, Burghers and Peasants) were required to carry through a parliamentary decision. Sitting beside a little park to the east of Senate Square is the House of Nobility (Ritarihuone), a brick building with Gothic influences that dates from 1862. This house was built as a meeting place for the Noble Estate, and members of the Finnish aristocracy still occupy it today.

The three non-noble Estates had to share premises: the **House of Estates** (1890), behind the cathedral on Snellmaninkatu, was their meeting place. The frieze on the tympanum depicts Emperor Alexander I surrounded by the heads of the Four Estates and the symbols of faith and justice.

The internationally acclaimed Kamppi Chapel of Silence

the most influential figure in Finnish history from the Civil War to the late 1940s. Helsinki has a museum dedicated to his memory (see page 56).

Majestic buildings line either side of the street – mainly modern on one side and traditional on the other – with many of Finland's major political and cultural institutions, such as its Parliament and the National Museum, among them.

KAMPPI

Just off the southern end of Mannerheimintie is **Kamppi**, a busy shopping and travel centre, containing two underground bus stations and a Metro station. Take a moment away from the rushing crowds and step into another of Helsinki's one-of-a-kind churches. The award-winning **Kamppi Chapel of Silence** ⓬ (tel: 050 578 1136; Mon–Fri 10am–5pm; www.kampinkappeli.fi) is an astonishing building, constructed from curving strips of spruce.

Over the road, on Yrjönkatu, is the **Amos Anderson Art Museum** ⓭ (tel: 040 137 0700; Wed 4–8pm, Sat 11am–5pm; no charge but booking essential; www.amosanderson.fi), the biggest private art collection in Finland. It is housed in the impressive 1913 home and offices of Amos Anderson (1878–1961), a businessman and philanthropist who owned several printing houses and *Hufvudstadsbladet* – the country's largest Swedish-language newspaper. He was an avid collector of twentieth-century Finnish art, and the works he amassed are on display. There are also eight to twelve temporary exhibitions held here every year.

Once you've looked round the museum, treat yourself to a cocktail and a panoramic view of the city from the **Ateljee Bar**, on the fourteenth floor of Sokos Torni Hotel next door.

Two 1930s Functionalist buildings can be found close to Kamppi. **Lasipalatsi** ("Glass Palace"), on Mannerheimintie, has been rejuvenated to create a welcoming media centre with an internet library; and **Tennispalatsi** ("Tennis Palace"), used for basketball matches during the 1952 Olympic Games, now houses Finland's largest cinema complex and the **Helsinki City Art Museum** ⓐ (Helsingin Taidemuseo Tennispalatsi; tel: 09 3108 7001; Tue 10am–5.30pm, Wed–Sun 11.30am–7pm; charge; www.helsingintaidemuseo.fi). The museum hosts interesting temporary exhibitions and has a section dedicated to Tove Jansson, of Moomins fame.

MANNERHEIMINTIE'S SIGHTS

Kiasma ⓑ (Kiasma, Nykytaiteen museo; Mannerheiminaukio 2, tel: 0294 500 501; Tues 10am–5pm, Wed–Fri 10am–8.30pm, Sat 10am–6pm, Sun 10am–5pm; charge, but free for under-18s; www.kiasma.fi), the city's museum of contemporary art is found in an amazing asymmetrical 1990s building, created by American architect Steven Holl and since completely renovated. The structure was designed to maximise the amount of light entering the building, and its oddly shaped windows also afford views of key landmarks. Its bold exhibitions of avant-garde Finnish and international contemporary art change three times per year. Outside, an impressive **equestrian statue** of Marshal Mannerheim is especially striking when illuminated at night.

At No. 30, the stately **Finnish Parliament Building** ⑯, with its fourteen Corinthian columns and a wide set of steps, was constructed in 1931 from the finest red Finnish granite. Arguably the best-known building in Finland, this is where the two hundred members of the Eduskunta, the Finnish legislature, meet. When in session, proceedings can be viewed from the public gallery.

Opposite Parliament is the music centre **Musiikkitalo** ⑰ (tel: 020 707 0400; www.musiikkitalo.fi), the home of the Helsinki

Kiasma, Helsinki's reigning museum of contemporary art

Philharmonic Orchestra, the Finnish Radio Symphony Orchestra and the Sibelius Academy. Its understated architecture is deliberate – it was designed to blend in rather than compete with its prestigious neighbours. The acoustics of its six concert halls, however, are second to none – Japanese acoustician Yasuhisa Toyota created each one to host a specific kind of music, from early music to electronica. A new square, **Kansalaistori**, setting for the Taste of Helsinki food festival (see page 99), was also created to link the new building with Kiasma.

The attractive pink **Hakasalmi Villa** ⑱ (tel: 09 3107 8519; Tue 11am–7pm ,Wed–Sun 11am–5pm; charge but free last Fri of every month and under-18s; http://hakasalmivilla.fi) sits unobtrusively in a pleasant English garden set back from the road. It was built in 1846 and was once the home of a wealthy benefactor, Aurora

The National Museum of Finland, guarded by a stone bear

Karamzin, who died here in 1902. Today it is a branch of the City Museum, holding changing art, history and folklore exhibitions throughout the year. At the time of writing, the Museum was under renovation and may not fully reopen until 2026/27.

The eye-catching façade and tower of the **National Museum of Finland** ⑲ (Suomen kansallismuseo; tel: 295 33 6000; Tues–Sun 11am–6pm; charge, but free Fri 4–6pm; www.kansallismuseo.fi), built in National Romantic style to resemble a medieval church or castle, dates from the early 1900s. Its huge metal bears are guarded by a stone bear, an important national symbol, while inside the entrance hall ceiling is decorated with scenes from the Kalevala, painted by Akseli Gallen-Kallela. The exhibits themselves detail the development of Finnish life from the prehistoric era to present times, and are divided into six departments: "Prehistory of Finland" is the country's largest permanent archaeological exhibition; "Treasure Troves" is a sparkling collection of coins, medals, decorations, silver and weapons; "Realm – Swedish rule" and "Realm – Swedish and Russian rule" detail Finnish culture and society from the Middle Ages to the nineteenth century; "A Land and its People" documents life before industrialisation; and "Suomi Finland" investigates daily twentieth-century living. The collection of the former **Museum of Cultures**, documenting different peoples of the world, is also found here. On the third floor is an interactive exhibition for children (see page 99).

NATURAL HISTORY MUSEUM AND TEMPPELIAUKIO CHURCH

A large bronze elk (made by one of the museum's taxidermists) hints at the contents of the distinguished neo-baroque building standing 300m (328 yards) along Arkadiankatu. The **Finnish Museum of Natural History** ⑳ (Luomus; tel: 02941 28800; Tues–Sun 10am–5pm, winter closed Monday; charge; www.luomus.fi)

Temppeliaukion Church is built into the rock

contains a small but interesting collection of bones and some vivid taxidermy dioramas. Pick up a free headset for English explanations.

Kunsthalle Helsinki 🛈 (tel: 040 450 7211; Tues, Thurs, Fri 11am–6pm, Wed 11am–8pm, Sat–Sun 11am–5pm; charge; http:// taidehalli.fi) has no collections of its own, but hosts six to eight major contemporary art exhibitions, curated from studios, galleries and museums elsewhere, every year. Retrospectives of esteemed Finnish (Eero Saarinen, Alvar Aalto) and international (Arne Jacobsen, Helmut Newton, Andy Warhol, Anish Kapoor) figures have been held here; the hall also promotes the work of up-and-coming artists.

Continue a further 300m/yards northwest to find one of Helsinki's most famous tourist attractions. The **Rock Church** 🛈 (Temppeliaukion kirkko; tel: 09 2340 6320; open daily but check tel. 09 2340 6320 for opening hours; www.temppeliaukionkirkko.

fi) is an architectural oddity, quarried out of solid bedrock. The inner stone walls are topped by a massive copper dome with a diameter of 24m (79ft). It is lined with 22km (13 miles) of copper stripping, and light is reflected inwards from 180 skylights. It can hold a congregation of nearly one thousand and is a popular concert venue due to its excellent acoustics. Designed by the architect brothers Timo and Tuomo Suomalainen, the church was hugely controversial when it opened in 1969, but now attracts up to eight thousand visitors a day in summer. It's a good idea to come first or last thing in the day to avoid the worst crowding.

CITY PLANNING, HELSINKI STYLE

In the 1950s, an ambitious development plan, overseen by Alvar Aalto, was made to transform Töölönlahti Bay and the strip of land directly to its south into a utopian cultural and recreational area, lined with landmark public buildings. In the event, Finlandia Hall (1971) was the only structure to appear, at the southern end of the lake. However, twenty years later, the City of Helsinki resurrected the idea of turning the bay into a "living room" for its citizens. Finlandia Hall was joined by the Opera House (1993), Kiasma (1998) and Musikkitalo (2011). In 2016, the striking timber clad Löyly public sauna and restaurant was the trigger for the regeneration of the industrial Hernesaari harbourside. The latest project completed is the new Oodi Helsinki Central Library (oodihelsinki.fi). An international competition was launched in 2012 to choose a design, with the winning proposal "Käännös" selected in January 2014. Designed by ALA Architects, the three-storey building is a dreamy creation of glass and twisted Siberian larch timbers that looks as though it is floating in air.

TÖÖLÖNLAHTI BAY AND THE OLYMPIC STADIUM

Töölönlahti Bay is a wonderful thing to see in a capital city. Black-headed gulls hover like hummingbirds over its glinting waters before diving for fish, and a popular walking path runs through the surrounding Hesperia Park.

The plan was always for the bay to form the centre of a large cultural area. Directly by the waterside is the modernist **Finlandia Hall** ㉓ (tel: 09 40 241; www.finlandiatalo.fi) one of Finland's most iconic buildings. This masterpiece was designed, right down to the doorknobs, by renowned Finnish architect Alvar Aalto in 1962. However, since its completion in 1971, bitter Finnish winters have warped the Carraran marble used to create its striking white exterior, and leaps in acoustic technology have seen the Musiikkitalo (2011) take over as the country's pre-eminent venue for classical music. At the time of writing, the inside was closed for renovations until 2025, but when it reopens it'll be more accessible to the public with pedestrian walkways and a terraced café overlooking the bay.

Café overlooking the bay and Finlandia Hall

Next to the hall is the small **Hakasalmi Park**, whose main feature is a stainless-steel pool that is illuminated from below.

The four bronze hands on top of high posts behind the pool are a monument to Urho Kekkonen, President of Finland from 1956 to 1981, whose name is engraved in a rock behind the pool. The president was known for often using his hands to express himself, and even wrote exclusively by hand rather than with a typewriter.

At the end of the park is another impressive modern structure – considered Finnish architecture at its finest. Regular opera performances were held in Finland for one hundred and twenty years before the **Finnish National Opera ㉔** (Helsinginkatu 58; tel: 09 4030 2211; www.operafin.fi) moved to its new home here in 1993. There are performances of opera, ballet or classical music six nights a week – original-language performances are subtitled in Finnish, Swedish and English.

Beyond the northern end of Töölönlahti Bay, the **City Winter Garden** (Hammarskjöldintie 1, tel: 09 3103 9985; Mon–Thurs & Sat–Sun 10am–4pm; free) is a particularly peaceful haven. Established in 1893 it consists of a small formal garden with statuary, with pheasants running around, and a large, decorative greenhouse featuring an attractive combination of exotic plants, a fishpond and various pieces of modern art. The rose garden opens daily from 7am to 9pm in summer.

The most dominant structure by far is the 72m (236ft) tower of the **Olympic Stadium ㉕** (tel: 050 343 1619; Mon–Fri 8am–9pm, Sat 10am–5pm, Sun noon–5pm; charge for tower climb and guided tours; www.stadion.fi), and a visit to the two-level caged-in observation platform is recommended. The views are, quite simply, the finest in Helsinki and offer a panoramic perspective of the city and its surrounding archipelago.

Finland's excellent results in the Olympics of the 1920s led to dreams of holding the games in Helsinki. The city bid to be the 1940 host country, and the stadium, deemed to be one of the most beautiful in the world, was inaugurated on June 2, 1938. However, the Games were postponed due to World War II, and Helsinki did not get to host them until 1952. The stadium set its capacity record of 70,435 people during the competition; today it is still in use, pulling in up to forty thousand people for international sporting and musical events.

Also within the stadium complex is the **Sports Museum of Finland** (Urheilumuseo; tel: 09-434 2250; Mon, Tue & Fri 10am–6pm, Wed–Thurs 10am–7pm, Sat–Sun 11am–5pm; www.urheilumuseo.fi). It has thirty thousand multimedia exhibits and more than two hundred thousand photographs depicting great moments – both of victory and defeat – in the history of Finnish athletics. In front of the stadium a nude **statue of Paavo Nurmi** (1897–1973) celebrates one of the greatest of all Finnish athletes.

THE FLYING FINN

Sisu is a quality that the Finns pride: it conjures up toughness, independence, and grisly determination in the face of adversity. Paavo Nurmi (1897–1973), a middle- and long-distance runner, was the personification of *sisu*. A multiple world record-breaker, Nurmi won nine Olympic gold medals and three silvers in his twelve Olympic races, and is still remembered today for his extraordinary running style, speed and tough character.

Nurmi had running in his blood from an early age. Although his father, a religious man, disapproved of such a frivolous pastime, Nurmi exerted his independence and spent every spare moment running with boys in his neighbourhood and alone in the woods. At a time when the fledgling Finnish republic was struggling to build a cohesive identity, Nurmi came to be its sporting ambassador, winning worldwide admiration and acclaim as the Flying Finn.

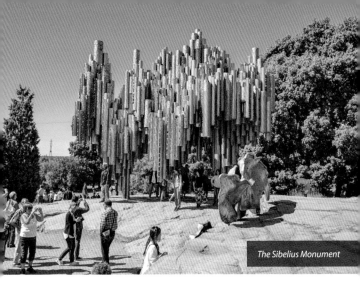

The Sibelius Monument

The **Sibelius Monument** 🄴 (1967) is a much-visited memorial dedicated to the revered Finnish composer, Jean Sibelius. Created by Eila Hiltunen, it consists of over six hundred welded steel tubes and weighs a whopping 24 tonnes. It is located in the pleasant Sibelius Park in the northwestern Taka-Töölö district.

THE "DESIGN DISTRICT"

When Helsinki became World Design Capital in 2012, the city invested heavily in promoting Finnish design. The "Design District" is an area of twenty five streets south of the Central Railway Station, containing almost two hundred designer boutiques, studios, galleries and museums. It centres around the Design Museum and the Museum of Finnish Architecture, and touches four districts, Kaartinkaupunki, Kamppi, Punavuori and Ullanlinna. A map of the Design District is available from the tourist office. Even if you aren't in the mood for shopping, there are plenty of interesting sights to see in this bohemian area.

ART AND ARCHITECTURE

The **Design Museum** ㉗ (Designmuseo; tel: 09 622 0540; June–Aug daily 11am–6pm, Oct–May closed Mon; charge; www.design museum.fi) focuses on industrial art and design and artistic handicrafts, with a permanent collection of more than 75,000 design objects, from the second half of the nineteenth century to the present. If you love Alvar Aalto, Kaj Franck, Oiva Toikka, Eero Saarinen, Tapio Wirkkala and others of their ilk, this is the place to see their work close-up.

Just behind the museum, at Kasarmikatu 24, is the moderately interesting **Museum of Finnish Architecture** (Suomen Rakennustaiteen museo; tel: 045 7731 0474; Tues, Thurs–Sun 11am–6pm, Wed 11am–8pm; charge; www.mfa.fi) in a neo-Renaissance building that was originally constructed for the Learned Societies in 1899.

Diagonally opposite is the neo-Gothic silhouette of **St John's Church** ㉘ (Johanneksen kirkko; Korkeavuorenkatu 12; tel: 09 2340 7730; summer Mon–Fri 10am–3pm, Sun for mass; www. helsinginkirkot.fi), the largest church in Helsinki, with its two piercing stiletto spires. Towards the end of the nineteenth century the growing population of Helsinki rendered the cathedral and the Old Church inadequate, and this third Lutheran place of worship was built. It has excellent acoustics and is a particular favourite for choral concerts.

Another impressive building is the **Mikael Agricola Church** ㉙ (1935) (Mikael Agricolan kirkko; tel: 09 2340 6123; Mon–Tue & Thurs 9am–3pm, Fri 9am–2pm, Sun for mass), designed by Lars Sonck in a mix of Art Nouveau and classical styles and easily identified by its hypodermic-like 30m (98 ft) spire. The spike can be retracted into the tower using a series of pulleys: this was done in World War II to confuse Russian bombers. Architecture fans might like to continue down Tehtaankatu, turning right into **Huvilakatu**, which contains some of the most attractive Art Nouveau houses in the city.

Huvilakatu

BULEVARDI AND HIETALAHTI MARKET

Beginning where Esplanadi stops, **Bulevardi** is an impressive street containing beautiful late nineteenth- and early twentieth-century buildings. Near its northeastern end you'll find Helsinki's oldest church, called, appropriately enough, the **Old Church ③** (Vanha kirkko; Lönnrotinkatu 6; tel: 09 2340 6128; Tue–Thurs noon–3pm). The church is Engel-designed but was only supposed to be a temporary structure until the new cathedral was ready. It was thrown together in 1826 using planks of wood and was never given any bells. However, by the time the cathedral was consecrated 26 years later, the city's population had increased so much that the Old Church was retained as a permanent place of worship. The church sits in a beautiful if macabre park: two-thirds of Helsinki's population were buried here in 1710, following an outbreak of plague.

Further down the street, in its own cobbled block, is the elegant **Alexander Theatre** (tel: 09 676 980; www.aleksanterinteatteri.fi). Named after Tsar Alexander II, it was built voluntarily by Russian officer engineers and conscripted soldiers and staged its first

Hietalahti Flea Market

performance in 1879. Today it is the site of many concerts, musicals and stage performances, mostly in Finnish.

The Sinebrychoff brewery, dating from 1819, once sat at the end of Bulevardi. It relocated in the early 1990s, but its name is preserved in the **Sinebrychoff Art Museum** ❸ (Sinebrychoffin taidemuseo; tel: 09 1733 6460; Tue, Thurs and Fri 11am–6pm, Wed 10am–8pm, Sat–Sun 10am–5pm; charge; www. sinebrychoffintaidemuseo.fi). This three-storey, Empire-style house was donated to the state by Paul and Fanny Sinebrychoff in 1921, along with its collections of Old Flemish, Dutch, Italian and French paintings, Swedish portraits, Russian icons, silver, china and antique furniture.

Directly across the road, **Hietalahti Market Hall** ❸ (Mon–Thurs 8am–9pm, Fri–Sat 8am–11pm, Sun 10am–5pm; www.hietalah denkauppahalli.fi) is an Art Nouveau structure, now a café and restaurant space with food from around the world. Outside, in summer, you will find just about everything up to, and including, the kitchen sink at **Hietalahti Flea Market** (Sat & Sun 10am–3pm) as well as global street food.

ALONG THE WATERSIDE

The **Cable Factory** ❸ (Tallberginkatu 1; tel: 09 4763 8300; www. kaapelitehdas.fi) cultural centre is located in converted U-shaped warehouses, out on the west of Helsinki. Nokia's former stamping ground houses an array of cultural facilities, including three esoteric museums, twelve galleries, and numerous art and music studios. Most people come here for specific shows and festivals: take a look at the website for upcoming events. Take the Metro to the Ruoholahti stop, from where the centre is a 600m (656 yards) walk.

ULLANLINNA AND KAIVOPUISTO

South of Market Square are two well-heeled districts, Ullanlinna and Kaivopuisto, composed of pretty parkland, stately embassies and beautiful old homes. Both offer a tranquil escape from the hustle and bustle of the city, making them popular spots.

Cable Factory

OBSERVATORY HILL

Tähtitorninmäki – which literally means "star-tower hill" – is an attractive park that rises above the northeastern end of Ullanlinna, allowing for views over the South Harbour. At the top you'll find an astronomy exhibition inside **Helsinki Observatory** ❸❹ (tel: 02 941 24244; Fri–Sat noon–4pm, Thurs noon–8pm; www.observatorio. fi), another Engeö-designed building whose revolving observation tower tested the architect's ingenuity.

Around the base of the hill, the formidable **Russian Embassy & Consulate** commands a whole block and was built in 1952 as part of Finland's war reparations to the Soviet Union. Opposite is the **Cathedral of St Henry** (Pyhän Henrikin Katedraali; Pyhän Henrikin aukio 1; tel: 09 637 853; http://henrik.katolinen.fi), built in neo-Gothic style. One of Helsinki's two Catholic churches, it was

Kaivopuisto Park

originally opened in 1860 as a garrison church. Nearby is Robert Stigell's bronze memorial, the **Statue of the Shipwrecked**, a well-known landmark.

KAIVOPUISTO PARK

Helsinki's favourite green space is **Kaivopuisto Park** ③. In summer, the city sponsors free concerts here, and Kaivopuisto overflows with happy locals, sunbathing, picnicking, strolling, and admiring the fine views across to Suomenlinna.

It's hard to believe that the park was a wasteland until the 1830s. At this time, Russians were forbidden to travel outside the empire, so for relaxation the upper classes were taken by steamer to enjoy the delights of Helsinki, St Petersburg and Tallinn. High-flying businessman Henrik Borgström cashed in on the situation by developing the cosmopolitan Kaivohuone spa on the headland. However, the Crimean War in the 1850s, and the subsequent lifting of the ban on foreign travel, soon brought this ritzy era to an end. The former spa, dating from 1838, now houses a restaurant.

The most ornate of the Empire-era **villas** sits on the corner of Kalliolinnantie and Itäinen Puistotie. It dates from 1839 and is the oldest preserved building in the park.

At Kalliolinnantie 8, the delightful wooden villa with the octagonal tower houses the **Cygnaeus Gallery** ③ (tel: 09 4050 9628; closed for renovation since 2014 but will reopen when funding becomes available), the oldest art museum in Finland. Its main exhibition consists of a nineteenth-century collection of Finnish art donated to the country by poet and critic Fredrik Cygnaeus (1807–81), professor of aesthetics and literature at Helsinki University.

Nearby, the more formidable building at Kalliolinnantie 14 belonged to one of Finland's most enigmatic and revered men, the Marshal of Finland Baron Carl Gustav Mannerheim (see page

19). The fascinating **Mannerheim Museum** ❸ (tel: 09 635 443; Fri–Sun 11am–4pm; charge for prebooked guided tours only; www.mannerheim-museo.fi) is housed in the 1870s Borman Villa, where Mannerheim once lived. Opened in 1951, and preserved as it was at Mannerheim's death, the exhibits include uniforms, medals and other personal memorabilia, as well as his extensive East Asian collections. The engaging guides do a great job of bringing his complex character to life.

SEA VIEWS

The highest point in the park is the tiny **Ursa Observatory**, from where there are fabulous panoramic views (in winter, the observatory hill is also Helsinki's prime sledging spot!). At the end of the park, **Café Ursula** (tel: 09 652 817; Sun–Thurs 9am–9pm, Sat–Sun

Café Ursula offers cake and fabulous sea views

9am–11pm; www.ursula.fi) is a Helsinki institution. Stop for coffee and cake, and of course to linger on the canopied terrace, with its stunning views of Suomenlinna and the other small islands offshore.

KALLIO AND AROUND

Kallio in film

Director Aki Kaurismäki plays with the realities and stereotypes of the working-class Kallio district in some of his films, most notably *Calamari Union* (1985), where fourteen men named Frank set off on a deadly journey from Kallio to Eira, an upmarket neighbourhood in the south of the city.

Ten minutes' walk from the ceaseless crowds at the Central Railway Station is an oasis of green tranquillity. **Kaisaniemi Botanic Garden** ㊳ (Kaisaniemenranta 2, tel: 09 1912 4455;; garden, daily 9am–8pm; free; greenhouses, Tues–Sun 10am–5pm, Thurs until 6pm June–Aug, to 4pm, Thurs until 6pm Sept–May; charge; www.luomus.fi) was actually established in Turku, and transferred to Helsinki's venerable Kaisaniemi Park in 1829. It consists of a formal garden with several 1830s Empire-style buildings and a series of greenhouses, the largest of which is the 1889 Palm House. The plants – nearly three thousand varieties – are grouped according to their family or origin; they are labelled white for basic plants, red for endangered ones, and yellow for edible and medicinal types.

Crossing over the Long Bridge – actually rather short – at the north side of the park brings you into the interesting, working-class area of **Kallio**.

HAKANIEMI MARKET

To the left of McDonald's you will see the statue of *The Boxers* by Johannes Haapasalo, and in the large square to the right is

Hakaniemi Market ⓷⓽ (Mon–Sat 6.30am–3pm), with an enticing array of products ranging from vegetables and fish to wicker furniture. There are also some of the small, tented cafés that are so popular across Finland. The two-storey **Market Hall** (Mon–Sat 8am–6pm; www.hakaniemenkauppahalli.fi) has food on the lower level, and an array of textiles and souvenirs upstairs. Unlike the Old Market Hall by Market Square, this one caters more to local people than to tourists.

KALLIO CHURCH

The most dominant landmark is straight ahead on top of the hill, reached by the longest street in Helsinki, Siltasaarenkatu. Before starting the climb, note the unusual memorial to the left at the first intersection. It consists of a leaning 8m (26 ft) steel tower and a 7.5m (24.5 ft) slab of grey Kuru granite, with reliefs depicting women at work in homes, factories and farms, and is the first national memorial honouring the work done by women during World War II.

The tall, granite, Art Nouveau tower of **Kallio Church** ⓸⓪ (Kallion kikko, tel: 09 2340 3620; Mon–Fri 7am–9pm, Sat–Sun 9am–7pm; www.helsinginkirkot.fi) is most impressive, and sits on one of Helsinki's highest spots. Consecrated on 1 September 1912, it is the only church in Finland that has both baroque and French Romantic organs. It also has seven bells, and Sibelius composed a melody especially for them; it was used by the Finnish Broadcasting Company for a number of decades, when they were rung on Saturday evening. It's rung in the church at noon and 6pm.

SORNÄINEN

Areas of the industrial Sornäinen district, northeast of Kallio, are being slowly transformed into cultural spaces. The former power station **Suvilahti** makes an epic backdrop for rock and metal gigs, such as the Tuska Open-Air Metal Festival (www.tuska-festival.fi) held at the end of June. Its old industrial units are being rented out to various cultural groups as office and exhibition spaces. **Cirko – Centre for New Circus** (www.cirko.fi), based in a former gasworks, has a year-round programme of contemporary Finnish circus performances. Kalasatama metro station is right next door to the power station.

LENININPUISTO AND LINNANMÄKI

Lenininpuisto is a pleasant little park with a much broader array of trees and shrubs than you would normally find in a Finnish garden, the result of a garden exhibition that was held here in 1961–62. The park was originally named Alpine Park (Alppipuisto), but was

Flow Festival in Suvilahti

The impressive Suomenlinna Fortress

given a new moniker in 1970, the one hundredth anniversary of Vladimir Ilyich Lenin's birth, as a friendly nod to the Soviet Union.

Helsinki's amusement park, **Linnanmäki** ⓐ (tel: 010-5722 200; May–mid-Oct: days and times vary – see website for details; www. linnanmaki.fi), is perched on top of a wooded hill. Half a million people visit every year, attracted by its rides and sideshows, from an old-fashioned carousel to the famous wooden rollercoaster Vuoristorata to up-to-date rides like the 75m- (246 ft-) tall freefall tower Kingi. A few of the rides are free; an all-ride pass costs €47, with profits going to children's charities.

You can also buy a joint ticket (€47) that covers entry to Linnanmäki and its neighbour, **Sea Life Helsinki** (tel: 09-565 8200; May–Aug daily 10am–7pm, June and July until 8pm; Sept–Apr Mon–Tues and Thurs–Sun 10am–5pm, Wed 10am–7pm; charge; www.visitsealife.com/helsinki). The Sea Life centre is fairly small, but it has been extremely well designed, and the staff are knowledgeable. Different tank's feeding times take place on the hour – check details online or as you enter.

If you have small children whose legs need a rest, Linnanmäki and Sea Life Helsinki are served by tram Nos 3 and 9, and bus No. 23, from the Central Railway Station.

SUOMENLINNA FORTRESS

Suomenlinna Fortress ⓬ is one of the biggest sea forts in the world, with fortifications scattered across eight rocky skerries. It is Helsinki's top attraction, as well as being a Unesco World Heritage Site, and deserves a full day to explore. The municipal HSL ferry (www.hsl.fi departs year-round from the pier in front of the Presidential Palace near Market Square, landing at the Main Quay on the north side of Iso Mustasaari Island. It is supplemented in summer by FRS Finland Oy's waterbus (www.frs-finland.fi), which also departs from Market Square from the "Lüypekinlaituri" Pier, landing at the Suomenlinna Centre pier on the south of Iso Mustasaari, and at King's Gate on Kustaanmiekka. The ferry ride takes fifteen to twenty minutes and usually run until after midnight.

The **Suomenlinna Centre** (May–Sept daily 10am–6pm, Oct–Apr daily 10.30am–4.30pm; www.suomenlinna.fi), on the south of Iso Mustasaari, is the place to pick up a copy of the colourful and practical guide to the islands, or to join one of the guided tours (in English: June–Aug two daily, late morning and early afternoon, May & Sept Fri–Sat 10.30am, check website for times). There is also a **visitor centre** (tel: 029 533 8410; May–Sept daily 10am–6pm, Oct–Apr daily 10am–4pm) at the Main Quay, with brochures and an introductory exhibition.

Some paths are rather rough and difficult to access with wheelchairs or children's pushchairs – the visitor centre can also provide a map of routes suitable for those with impaired mobility. A torch will come in handy if you want to explore some of the tunnels that run underneath the fortification. Bring a swimsuit too, as there are several sheltered coves with little sandy beaches.

There are twelve cafés and restaurants on the islands, although some are summer only. For restaurants, see page 111. Café Piper (tel: 09-668 447; daily late May-mid-Sept 10.30am–5pm), in a park just south of the Ehrensvärd Crown Castle, offers alfresco dining with a stunning view.

Accommodation on the island is limited to Hostel Suomenlinna (see page 141).

CONSTRUCTION OF THE FORTRESS

By the middle of the seventeenth century Sweden had become one of the great European powers. However, this predominance began to slip after 1703, when Peter the Great founded the new Russian capital of St Petersburg and fortified its approaches with the naval base of Kronstadt. Successive wars saw Sweden lose much of its Baltic territories, and, through the treaties of Nystad and Turku, the Russian frontier was brought much closer, posing more of a threat. In 1748, the Swedish Diet approved a new naval base in Helsinki to protect its shipping channels.

The ferry to Suomenlinna

The new fortress, occupying a series of small islands outside Helsinki harbour, was called Sveaborg – Sweden's Fortress – and became the largest construction project ever undertaken by the country. Lieutenant-Colonel Augustin Ehrensvärd (1710–72), an astute politician and experienced fortress planner, had the responsibility of overseeing the construction. He decided that, to keep the edifice hidden as much as possible from enemy view, it should be a bastion with low fortification devices. It took many thousands of Finnish workers some forty years to complete the principal work – by which time the walls extended to a total of around 8km (5 miles), with enough room for 1,300 cannons.

MILITARY ACTION

By 1806, around 4600 people were living on Sveaborg (Suomenlinna), making it the second-largest city in Finland after Turku. In 1809, Finland became an autonomous duchy within the Russian Empire, ending the 600-year period of Swedish rule. It was the presence of this fortress that prompted the Russians to make Helsinki the new Finnish capital in 1812.

A period of peace followed. However, this was shattered by the Crimean War of 1854–56, during which an Anglo-French fleet shelled and badly damaged the fortress over a period of three days. After the war, extensive restoration work was undertaken, with new defensive work on the western and southern edges of the islands. In the build up to World War I the fortress and surrounding islands were incorporated into naval fortifications designed to protect St Petersburg.

After Finland gained its independence, Sveaborg was given its new name, Suomenlinna or "Finland's Fortress". Its first, grisly use was as a death camp for the Reds (communists) who had lost the Finnish Civil War. It was then utilised as a closed military zone until 1948, and it was not until 1973 that Suomenlinna received a civilian administration. In 1991 the fortress became a Unesco World Heritage Site, for its unique and excellently preserved military architecture.

ARTISTIC ENCLAVE

Despite its military purpose, Suomenlinna has always been known as a place of avant-garde culture, where the arts, music and theatre have flourished, an environment assisted by the large numbers of officers stationed there. Augustin Ehrensvärd himself had a passion for art, having studied painting, drawing and engraving in Paris in his 20s.

Today, many artists live permanently on Suomenlinna. There are a number of studios and galleries on the islands, including the Pot Viapori Ceramic Studio and the Hytti Glass Studio, where you can watch glass being blown. The three-day craft-focused Väkevä Viapori village fete is held in late October. Music and theatre also flourish: Suomenlinna has a vibrant jazz festival, the summertime Viapori Jazz (http://viaporijazz.fi), and the open-air summer theatre staged at the bastion of Hyvä Omatunto – meaning Good Conscience – regularly has sell-out performances.

There are around eight hundred civilians living on the islands now, of whom about four hundred work here year round, while the rest commute to Helsinki. They all enjoy a privileged position, being close to the centre of Helsinki yet removed from city stresses on their own idyllic islands.

SUOMENLINNA'S MUSEUMS

A visit to Suomenlinna is also enhanced by its collection of six museums, five of which are open only in summer. From June to August, you can purchase a combined admission ticket.

The most important is **Suomenlinna Museum** (Building C74, tel: 09 684 1850; May–Sept daily 10am–6pm; Oct–Apr daily

10.30am–4.30pm; charge). Located in the navy's former inventory chambers, it doubles as an information centre and details the history of the fortress from the eighteenth century to the present. Don't miss the interesting multimedia show, 'The Suomenlinna Experience', broadcast every half hour in the auditorium.

Suomenlinna artist at work

One of the oldest houses in the complex is the former Commandant's official residence, part home, part defensive structure – the crenellated dining-room window and sleeping alcove could be used to defend the fortress's main entrance in emergencies. It now houses the **Ehrensvärd Museum** (Building B40, tel: 09 684 1850; June–Aug daily 10.30am–5.30pm, late May and early Sept daily 11am–4pm; charge), containing portraits, furnishings and model ships. Ehrensvärd himself is buried in front of the house, his final resting place marked by an elaborate grave topped with a sword, shield and helmet that was designed by his godson, King Gustav III of Sweden.

The Military Museum has two separate entities. The **Manege** (Maneesi; Building C77, tel: 029 953 0261; May–Sept daily 11am–6pm; charge) features heavy military equipment – most of which dates from the World War II era – in an artillery storehouse constructed by the Russians in 1881. The **Submarine Vesikko** (*Sukellusvene Vesikko*; Building B79, tel: 029 953 0260;

Submarine Vesikko

early-May–Sept daily 11am–6pm; charge), which patrolled the Gulf of Finland during the Winter and Continuation Wars, is the Finnish Navy's only surviving WWII submarine.

A more gentle experience can be found at the **Toy Museum** (Lelumuseo; Building C66, tel: 040 500 6607; June–Aug 11am–6pm, late April–mid-May and Sept weekends only, check website for times; charge, prebooking necessary; www.lelumuseo.fi) where, in an old Russian villa, there is a collection of dolls and toys dating from the 1830s onwards. There's also a small café, should you need a break for refreshment.

The tiny **Customs Museum** (Building B20 D, tel: 040 332 2774; June–Aug Tues–Sun 12.30pm–5.30pm; free; http://tulli.fi) on Susisaari has an exhibition on customs and smuggling. Plan your visit to coincide with a sunny day to fully enjoy the outdoor attractions that this beautiful island has to offer such as relaxing on the shores of the Gulf of Finland or a nature walk to complete the day.

SUOMENLINNA CHURCH

Not to be missed is **Suomenlinna Church** (Suomenlinnan kirkko; tel: 09 2340 6126; summer Mon–Thurs 10am–4pm, Fri 10am–1pm), which was inaugurated in 1854 as the Alexander Nevsky Orthodox Church. Originally, it had five towers with onion domes but when, in 1928, it changed alliances and became a Lutheran church, four of the towers were demolished and the main one rebuilt in more fitting style. Its bell is the largest in Finland and the fence, made of cannon and chains, was erected in the 1850s. The church is popular for summer weddings, and also functions as a lighthouse.

HELSINKI'S ISLANDS

Hundreds of islands dot the city's coastline. Some, like Lauttasaari and Kulosaari, have been so integrated by bridges and metro lines that they are almost indistinguishable from the mainland. Others are private, reserved for weekend cottages, reached over the ice in winter or by motorboat in summer. But others are recreational areas, open to all – the most famous being the great fortifications of Suomenlinna. Below are some other good choices.

SEURASAARI

A must-see sight, Seurasaari is a beautiful green park-like island, attached to the mainland by a wooden footbridge. You could spend a very happy afternoon here, exploring the appealing **Seurasaari Open-Air Museum** ⓭ (tel: 0295 33 6912; Jun–mid-Sept 11am–5pm; charge) and its forested surroundings. The museum was founded in 1909 and has 86 traditional buildings – cottages, farmsteads, a church and parsonage and a manor house – relocated from all Finland's provinces, which give visitors an engaging perspective of Finnish rural life from the eighteenth to the twentieth century. Guides in traditional costumes demonstrate craft skills and folk dancing, and an optional guided tour (in English at 3pm) is included in the ticket price. Helsinki's main Midsummer's Eve celebrations take place here in June: the national flag flutters over traditional dancers, a merry wedding and a huge bonfire. A bonfire is also lit here on Easter Saturday, to drive away witches and evil spirits, who are said to be particularly active on that day.

On the western side of the island is the pretty **Seurasaari Beach**, created in 1906. It mainly functions as a naturist beach, with separate areas for women and men, but swimsuits are compulsory on Wednesday and Sunday.

Bus No. 24 runs to Seurasaari from the western end of Esplanadi. The pleasant route takes you around the waterside, past Sibelius Park, and gives you a glimpse of **Mäntyniemi**, the official residence of the Finnish president.

KORKEASAARI

Korkeasaari, a rocky outcrop offshore from the Mustikkamaa district of Helsinki, has served time as farmland, a timber store and as a military zone, but since 1889, it has been the home of **Helsinki Zoo** ㊹ (Högholmen; tel: 09-310 37900; daily May–Aug 10am–8pm, Mar–Apr and Sept until 6pm, Oct–Feb until 4pm; charge; www.korkeasaari.fi). Perhaps not surprisingly, this popular tourist attraction specialises in "cold climate animals", including some big beasts like Asian lions, brown bear and snow leopards – the zoo has a very successful breeding programme for the latter. The interesting Amazonia House enclosure is home to South American animals. Feeding times are listed on the website. Bus No. 16 runs from the Central Railway Station year-round; but if you're here in summer, it's great fun to go by boat. A JT (www.jt-line.fi) service runs daily from Market Square May to

Saaristo, one of many island-restaurants

September. Less scenically the Kalasatama metro stop is about 1km from the entrance.

PIHLAJASAARI

Helsinki's favourite island for swimming is undoubtedly **Pihlajasaari** ("Rowan Island"), actually two islands joined by a bridge. You'll find a sandy beach, café, sauna and changing cabins on the larger island's western shore. The mixed naturist beach is on the smaller island, which also hides wartime bunkers. Pihlajasaari is just a ten-minute trip from the mainland. Boats depart from mid-May to August every fifteen to thirty minutes, from outside Café Carusel, at the western edge of Kaivopuisto Park. Weekend camping is also permitted, giving you plenty of time to take in the beautiful surroundings. To make the most of your visit, consider taking a leisurely stroll through the lush greenery, and don't forget to pack a picnic for a delightful *al fresco* dining experience.

HARAKKA

"Magpie Island" is now a wildlife reserve but, up until 1990, was used for military purposes; this helps explain why it is still so pristine. A network of paths (marked by signposts giving information in Finnish and Swedish) circle the tiny island, and visitors are asked not to stray from these paths or remove plants. There's lots of birdlife here, and an art centre with artists' studios. You can reach Harakka by boat in summer: to summon your craft, hoist the red-and-white wooden signal at the end of the Ullanlinna pier, near to Café Ursula in Kaivopuisto Park, and a boat should arrive within half an hour. Don't forget to bring your binoculars for some prime birdwatching. Whether you're an art enthusiast, a nature lover, or simply seeking a peaceful escape from the bustling city, Harakka Island has something special to offer.

Helsinki Zoo brown bear

GREATER HELSINKI

The Capital and Greater Helsinki areas spread out in a concentric fan shape around the central city. Their quiet commuter towns and suburbs hide several interesting sights.

TARVASPÄÄ

Akseli Gallén-Kallela (1865–1931) is considered by many to be Finland's greatest national artist. After studying at the Finnish Society of Fine Arts, he made his debut in the 1880s to popular acclaim, with his realistic images of everyday Finns. Gallén-Kallela became fascinated with Elias Lönnrot's epic poetry collection, the Kalevala, even honeymooning in the regions where the folk poems originated. His rich, romantic paintings revisit the poems' mythical heroes and their stories over and over again.

Gallén-Kallela designed and built a studio-home, **Tarvaspää** (1911–13), overlooking Laajalahti Bay 10km (6.2 miles) west of Helsinki, bringing to life his dream of "a crenellated castle, with a tower of grey stone and timbers of pine and oak". His studio has been converted into the **Gallén-Kallela Museum** (Gallén-Kallenlatie 27; tel: 010 406 8840; daily 11am–6pm, 8pm on Wed; charge; guided tours by arrangement; www.gallen-kallela.fi), a peaceful oasis consisting of a studio wing, tower and main building, with a coffee house and a terrace restaurant. The museum holds some one hundred illustrations for the *Kalevala*, which decorated the Finnish Pavilion at the Paris World Exhibition in 1900; the paintings themselves can be seen at the Ateneum in Helsinki (see page 28).

Tram No. 4 runs nearby from central Helsinki: get off at Laajalahti aukio and enjoy the scenic 2km (1-mile) walk to the museum through Munkinpuisto Park, where you can pause for a moment of peace and tranquillity.

ESPOO

Populated largely by wealthier Finns who commute to Helsinki, Espoo is a strange mix of rural farm areas and genteel, leafy suburbs that offer a large and colourful palette of Finnish residential architectural styles. It is actually Finland's second-largest city, although it feels a planet away from the Londons or Tokyos of this world. In particular, Espoo's **Tapiola** area, named after Tapio, the *Kalevala's* spirit of the forest, is a renowned 1950s and 1960s planned garden suburb. Leading architects of the age aimed to create a harmonious mix of housing, cultural and recreational facilities, set around a central pool. **Espoo Cultural Centre** (Espoon kulttuurikeskus; www.espoo.fi/en/espoo-cultural-centre), home to the city's orchestra and theatre, and host of the big April Jazz Festival, sits at its heart. The white quartzite, concrete and glass complex was created in 1972 by Arto Sipinen, who worked with Alvar Aalto and has designed monumental-style civic works in the same tradition.

Another of Espoo's assets is **WeeGee** (tel: 09 816 31818, Wed–Fri 11am–7pm, Tue, Sat, Sun 11am–5pm; charge; www.weegee.fi), a clutch of five museums gathered inside an atmospheric old printing works. The best-known is **EMMA** (emmamuseum.fi), with around 2500 Finnish art works dating from the 1950s onwards. Finland's largest collection of West African objects, gathered by the radio and television reporter Helinä Rautavaara, can be seen in the interesting **ethnographic museum** (http://helinamuseo.fi), and the **Leikki – the Museum of Play** (Museo Leikki; museoleikki.fi/en) is also worth a look.

NUUKSIO NATIONAL PARK

Finns have a passion for the outdoors, and much of the Finnish landscape is safeguarded by 38 varied national parks. Just 16km (10 miles) north of Espoo is **Nuuksio National Park** (Nuuksion kansallispuisto; www.nationalparks.fi), a great place to come for a short hiking trip of a day or two. The park is one of the most important conservation areas in Finland, with cool, herb-rich forests, lakes and mires that are home to a number of threatened species, including the wood lark, European nightjar and various flying squirrels. Around 33km (20 miles) of marked trails thread through the area, and many companies offer activities such as fishing, canoeing and mushroom-picking in summer, and guided snowshoe walking and skiing excursions in winter – see the national park website for a full list of providers.

The award-winning **Finnish Nature Centre Haltia** (tel: 040 163 6200; May–Sept 10am–6pm, Oct–Apr Tue–Sat 10am–5pm; charge for exhibition; www.haltia.com) has exhibitions on Finnish nature. You can reach the park's eastern/northern trails from the centre

Espoo Museum of Modern Art

Hiking in the Nuuksio National Park

of Espoo via bus 245(A). During the summer season, a bus also runs from Helsinki – simply enquire at the tourist office for more information on the available bus services.

HVITTRÄSK

Hvitträsk (tel: 029 533 6951, www.kansallismuseo.fi; May–Sept daily 11am–5pm, Oct–Apr Wed–Sun 11am–5pm; charge; guided tours in May Sat–Sun, June–Sept Wed–Sun at 3pm), some 20km (14 miles) west of Helsinki in Kirkkonummi municipality, is another must-see mecca for anyone interested in Finnish art, architecture and design.

Eliel Saarinen, Herman Gesellius and Armas Lindgren were three of Finland's most famous architects, responsible for many of Helsinki's most unusual and important buildings. Together they designed this studio home, where all three lived and worked. The stone and timber buildings, built in National Romantic style between 1901 and 1903, blend into the forest and cliffs, while the interior architecture, furniture and design form a harmonious whole.

Harmony of design did not always extend into the private lives of the little community, however. Saarinen's first wife, Matilda, crossed the garden to live with his partner, Gesellius. Apparently bearing her no grudge, Saarinen married Gesellius' sister, Loja, just two years later. But the triumvirate broke up in 1906, and by 1916 Saarinen was working at Hvitträsk on his own. In 1922, after winning a major prize in a competition in New York, Saarinen moved to the United States, becoming as well-known abroad as he was in Finland. He continued to visit Hvitträsk each year until his death in 1950, and his grave overlooks the lake that gave the house its name.

Hvitträsk can be reached by train (E, L, S or U train: Helsinki–Luoma; 6km/4-mile taxi ride).

EXCURSIONS

Helsinki is a small capital city: once you have seen its sights, take a day trip to soak up Finland's countryside; visit an atmospheric medieval trading town; or hop across the water to explore Tallinn, a Unesco World Heritage Site.

FISKARS

This attractive seventeenth-century ironworking village (*bruk*) makes for a very popular shopping/sightseeing trip from Helsinki. The village is where the Fiskars company, makers of the iconic, orange-handled tools, was born. A chuckling river runs in front of a long street of pretty buildings, many designed by Engel himself. Today, they form a concentrated pocket of Finnish art and design. Their little outlets, selling pottery, glassware, paper, leather goods, homeware, jewellery, clothing, chocolates and artisanal beer, open from 11am to 5pm in summer (weekends only during the rest of the year).

The Engel-designed **Clock Tower** building is the centrepiece of the village, containing an exhibition about the Fiskars company and a shop selling Fiskars products. Downriver, you'll find the nineteenth-century **copper forge** and **Assembly Hall**; while upstream near the lake is **Fiskars Museum** (Peltorivi 9, tel: 019 237 013; Sept–May Wed–Sun 11am–4pm; June–Aug daily 11am–5pm; charge; www.fiskarsmuseum.fi), a living-history museum, where costumed workers bring the village's ironworking history to life.

Mainly, the chief pleasure here lies in soaking up the charming atmosphere, wandering in and out of the studios and workshops, and stopping for cakes and coffee at one of the riverside cafés. All in all, Fiskars makes for a delightful day trip from Helsinki.

Red-ochre fishing cottages in Porvoo

Getting There

Fiskars is 88km (55 miles) west of Helsinki. Take the InterCity Helsinki-Turku train, and get off in Karjaa, from where the village is a twenty-minute bus ride (weekdays).

PORVOO (BORGÅ)

Finland's second-oldest town was once an affluent medieval trading centre, and many of its picturesque old buildings, including the ochre-red shore houses, have been preserved. Besides its fine cathedral, sitting on the hill between the Market Square and the riverside, the town has several interesting museums and speciality shops. Visit the **tourist office** (Läntinen Aleksanterinkatu 1; tel: 040 489 9801; daily 9am–3pm; www.visitporvoo.fi), based in the new Art Factory conference centre, to stock up on information.

The **Old Town** is a highlight of a visit to Porvoo. Down by the river, Jokikatu is a small, cobbled street with attractive wooden buildings housing an array of craft and souvenir shops. It is here that you really feel the ambience of this unusual little town, especially beside the old shore houses and granary buildings that back onto the river. One of these granaries now contains the **Porvoo Doll and Toy Museum** (tel: 040 501 5006; Jun–mid-Aug daily 10am–3pm; charge; www.lelumuseo.com), consisting of over 1,000 dolls and hundreds of toys collected from Finland and abroad. It is generally considered the best collection of its kind in the country.

The square, rococo-style Old Town Hall (1764), with an unusual central tower, is one of only two eighteenth-century town halls remaining in Finland. It contains works by two Porvoo natives, artist Albert Edelfelt (1854–1905) and the sculptor Ville Vallgren (1855–1940), who went on to win international fame – Vallgren's most famous work is the statue *Havis Amanda* (see page 29) in Helsinki. The rest of **Porvoo Museum** (tel: 040 197 5557; May–Aug Mon–Sat 10am–4pm, Sun 11am–4pm; Sept–Apr Wed–Sun noon–4pm; charge;

Colourful Porvoo

www.porvoonmuseo.fi), detailing bygone times with displays of costumes, textiles, glass, porcelain and silver, is in the neighbouring Holm House.

Steep, cobbled Sillanmäki – difficult for cars and pedestrians alike – leads up to one of Finland's loveliest Gothic churches, **Porvoo Cathedral** (Tuomiokirkko; tel: 019-661 1250; May–Sept Mon–Fri 10am–6pm, Sat 10am–2pm, Sun 2–5pm; Oct–Apr Tues–Sat 10am–2pm, Sun 2–4pm; www.porvoonseurakunnat.fi). Following Russia's defeat of Sweden, the Diet of Porvoo (1809), which established Finland as a Grand Duchy belonging to Russia, was held here. Dating mainly from the fifteenth century, the building has had many near misses over the centuries, most notably when it was hit by a bomb in World War II and damaged by arson in 2006. Points of interest include a statue of Alexander I, erected in 1909 on the centenary of the Porvoo Diet, and the cathedral's separate bell tower.

Finland's national poet J. L. Runeberg (1804–77) was a local lad – the town still celebrates his birthday on 5th February with an annual torchlight parade and jam-topped Runeberg tarts. On the other side of town, in a grid of Empire-style houses, you'll find Finland's oldest home museum, the **J. L. Runeberg Home** (tel: 040 489 9900; May–Aug daily 10am–4pm; Sept–Apr Wed–Sun 10am–4pm; charge). Runeberg and his family lived here for 25 years. In 1882, the building was opened as a museum, and the interior remains unchanged from that time.

Getting There

Porvoo is 50km (32 miles) east of Helsinki. There are bus services every half hour, departing from Kamppi bus station in Helsinki, taking around an hour.

Tallinn

If you prefer to go by boat, the *J. L. Runeberg* (tel: 040 548 9005, msjlruneberg.fi) sails in summer from Helsinki Market Square, leaving at 10am and returning at 4pm, allowing around 2.5 to 3 hours' sightseeing in Porvoo. It sets sail every day except Thursday in July and Tue–Wed, Fri–Sun in June and August (some other sailings available in May), with the return journey costing €47.

TALLINN, ESTONIA

Helsinki's central position on the Gulf of Finland makes it

an excellent jumping-off point for visits to other Baltic cities. Tallinn, the capital of Estonia, is the closest, just a 1.5-hour hop across the water. It is a popular destination for Finns, drawn by its lively nightlife. Tallinn's prosperity was built up during the thirteenth to sixteenth centuries, when it was the northernmost member of the Hanseatic trading league. Despite the centuries of turmoil that followed, the Old Town has survived relatively unscathed. A living medieval monument, it was made a Unesco World Heritage Site in 1997.

To get a sense of the city, join the **Tallinn Free Tour**, which departs at noon daily from outside the tourist office at Niguliste 2.

Raekoda Plats

Town Hall Square (Raekoda plats) has been Tallinn's marketplace and social centre for more than seven centuries. Dominating it

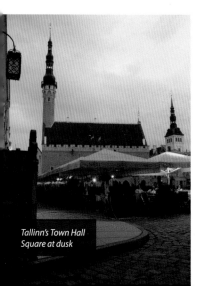

is the **Raekoda**, the oldest intact Gothic town hall in Northern Europe. Its eight-sided **tower** (tel: 645 7900; May–mid-Sept Mon–Thurs 11am–6pm, Fri-Sun 11am–4pm; charge; http://raekoda. tallinn.ee) has a viewing platform offering spectacular views. The **Old Thomas** (Vana Toomas) weathervane at the top of the tower was added in 1530.

Numerous interesting buildings line the square, and its cafés and restaurants are ideal places to soak up the city's engaging

Tallinn's Town Hall Square at dusk

at Raekoja plats 11, contains Europe's oldest **Chemist Shop** (tel: 631 4860; Mon–Sat 10am–6pm; www.raeapteek.ee), founded in 1422, which sells a marzipan concoction said to relieve the pain of love.

Church of the Holy Ghost

Just off the square, the **Church of the Holy Ghost** (tel: 646 4430; May–Sept Mon–Fri 9am–6pm, Sat and Sun between services, rest of year shorter, varied hours; charge; www.puhavaimu.ee) is easily identifiable by the attractive old clock – Tallinn's oldest – on its façade. The church dates from the fourteenth century and was built by the Order of the Holy Ghost. After the Reformation, the first sermons in the Estonian language were given here. The interior is richly decorated and includes one of the most precious medieval works of art in the country, an exquisite altar dating from 1483.

The church is almost on the corner of Pikk, a nice little street with an array of colourful stone houses. Particularly grand is the sixteenth-century **House of the Brotherhood of Blackheads** (tel: 5919 1414; www.mustpeademaja.ee), a guild for unmarried merchants. Today it is a popular concert venue.

At the junction with Pagari, the formidable building with bricked-up basement windows was the headquarters of the NKWD – better known by its later name, the KGB. Here, suspected enemies of the Soviet Union were interrogated, then shot or sent to Siberian work camps.

City Walls and the Cathedral

The Square of Towers Park has the best views of the formidable **City Walls** (Tallinna Linnaamüür). The walls encompassed 2.5km (1.5 miles), and about 75 percent still stand today. In the Middle Ages, there were six gates and no fewer than 66 towers. Today nineteen survive: the ones in this stretch are oddly shaped, and topped by irregular, conical, red-tiled roofs. Climb the nearby **Nun's Tower** (Nunna torn; tel: 644 9867; daily 11am–4pm; charge) and cross the wooden platform towards the Bath Tower and Golden Leg Tower (*Sauna* and *Kuldjala*).

On Castle Square (Lossi plats), **St Alexander Nevsky Cathedral** (tel: 644 3484; daily 8am–6pm, Sat till 7pm; free; https://nevsky sobor.ee) looms over the area, dominated by five unmistakable onion-shaped domes. Named in honour of the Russian duke who attacked southeastern Estonia in the first part of the thirteenth century, the cathedral was constructed between 1894 and 1900 on the orders of Tsar Alexander III. The bell tower contains Tallinn's grandest collection of bells, the largest weighing an impressive fifteen tonnes; the entire ensemble is played before each service. Standing as a symbol of architectural grandeur, St. Alexander

Al fresco lunch along Tallinn's Vana Turg

Nevsky Cathedral is a must-see landmark in Tallinn.

Toompea Castle

Opposite the cathedral's main entrance is the pink baroque façade of **Toompea Castle**, (Toompea loss; tel: 631 6331; exhibitions open Mon–Fri 10am–4pm; free; www.riigikogu.ee) emblazoned with the city's coat of arms – three lions on a gold background. The dominant feature of the castle is the battlemented, 46m (151ft)

Toompea Castle

fourteenth-century tower on the southwestern corner. Called **Pikk Hermann** (Tall Hermann), it is the symbol of Tallinn. After a 50-year Russian occupation, the blue, black and white tricolour, the national flag of Estonia, was raised here once again in 1991.

Take Toom-Kooli – between the cathedral and the castle – to the **Dome Church** (Toomkirik; tel: 644 4140; Tue–Sun 10am–4.30pm; free; http://toomkirik.ee). It dates from the time of the first Danish invaders in the thirteenth century, when it was just a wooden hall, dedicated to St Mary the Virgin. It is the oldest church on mainland Estonia, and the country's primary Lutheran church. The Gothic exterior dates from the fourteenth century.

Getting There

Ferries to Tallinn take about two hours with **Tallink Silja** (in Helsinki, tel: +358 9 180 41, in Tallinn, tel: +372 640 9808; www.tallinksilja.com), with at least six departures per day.

Saunas are generally same sex only; mixed ones are either for families or groups of close friends

THINGS TO DO

ENTERTAINMENT

Helsinki is full of music. Whether you enjoy classical concerts, or headbanging to heavy metal, or something in between, the city has something for you. State-of-the-art auditoriums host orchestras and operas; choral music crescendos in the city's churches; two distinguished theatres entertain in both Finnish and Swedish; and live music fills the city's pubs and clubs.

Helsinki may not have the biggest bar scene on earth, but its nightlife is friendly, vibrant and inclusive. Quirky pubs, designer bars, laidback jazz joints and wild nightclubs will keep you partying your way across town until the early hours.

Two national parks lie on Helsinki's doorstep, full of opportunities for outdoor activities and wildlife watching. Within the city, you can canoe, experience a Finnish sauna, sunbathe at the beach, or enjoy the passionate atmosphere at an ice hockey match.

CONCERT AND THEATRE TICKETS

Tickets can be booked through the following ticket agencies:

Lippupiste (Luckan Forum, Simonsgatan 8; tel: 0600 900 900 – local call charge plus €1.98 per minute; open Mon, Wed, Fri 11am–5pm, Tues, Thurs 11am–7pm, Sat noon–3pm; www.lippu.fi)

Ticketmaster (Mannerheimintie 13 a A; tel: 0600 10 800 – local call charge plus €1.98 per minute; open Mon–Fri 10am–5pm, Sat 11am–4pm; www.ticketmaster.fi)

Tiketti (Aleksanterinkatu 52; tel: 0600 900 900– local call charge plus €2 per minute; open Mon–Sat 9am–9pm, Sun 10am–6pm; tickets issued by any R-Kiosk around the city; www.tiketti.fi)

Mussikkitalo design

The seating in the Music Centre's main concert hall mimics logs floating down a Finnish river, while the traditional Finnish smoke sauna is conjured up in the auditorium's stained-birch woodwork.

MUSIC AND THEATRE

Finland has a lively **classical music** scene, with a disproportionately high number of world-class composers, conductors and performers. The state-of-the-art **Helsinki Music Centre** (Musiikkitalo; tel: 020 707 0400; www.musiikkitalo.fi) is Helsinki's newest music venue and home of the prestigious **University of the Arts** (www.uniarts.fi), the **Finnish Radio Symphony Orchestra** (www.yle.fi/rso) and the Helsinki Philharmonic Orchestra. The Centre hosts up to one hundred concerts per month between September and May, of mostly classical music but also hosts the occasional rock gig.

The **Rock Church** (Temppeliaukio; Lutherinkatu 3; tel: 09 2340 5940), hewn from solid bedrock, also has amazing acoustics. Chamber concerts, and jazz, choir and piano recitals are held here; performances of Sibelius's work are especially popular.

Finland has a long-standing love affair with opera. The recently renovated **Finnish National Opera** (Helsinginkatu 58; tel: 09 4030 2211; www.opera.fi) stages around fifteen classic and contemporary operas per season (September to May), plus nine ballets.

Kulttuuritalo (Sturenkatu 4; tel: 09 774 0270; www.kulttuuritalo.fi), opened in 1958, was architect Alvar Aalto's first public building in Helsinki. The asymmetrical auditorium has some of the best acoustics in the country, and hosts a year-round programme of pop, rock and classical concerts, as well as MMA fights and stand-up comedy shows.

Recently renamed after the Russian owners were sanctioned following Russia's invasion of Ukraine, **Helsinki Halli** (Areenakuja

1; tel. 204 1997), this major arena next to Pasila railway station, is currently closed but is expected to reopen to host major sporting events, shows and rock gigs. Purchase tickets from Lippupiste.

Finland's **UMO Jazz Orchestra** (http://umohelsinki.fi), a Finnish Big Band with 26 albums to its name, plays everything from boogie to the blues. The orchestra performs around eighty concerts per year at venues across the country and abroad – check the website for details. One of Europe's best jazz clubs, **Happy Jazz Club Storyville** (Museokatu 8; tel: 050 363 2664; www.storyville.fi) is an ever-popular Helsinki nightspot. Close to the parliament building, in an old coal cellar, you'll find live jazz from 7pm until the early hours Wednesday to Saturday. The ground-floor Piano Bar opens Tuesday to Saturday from 6pm, and in summer there is daily live music on the delightful Garden Terrace which opens at 2pm.

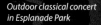

Outdoor classical concert in Esplanade Park

The **Finnish National Theatre** (Läntinen teatterikuja 1; tel: 010 733 1331; www.kansallisteatteri.fi) and the **Swedish Theatre** (Svenska Teatern; Pohjoisesplanadi 2; tel: 09 6162 1411; www.svenskateatern.fi) both enjoy long traditions of performance in, respectively, Finnish and Swedish. The National Theatre has English surtitles for some performances.

CINEMA

Finns do not dub foreign films, so you can enjoy newly released Hollywood movies at the ten-screen **Kinopalatsi** in Kaisaniemenkatu 2, and at Finland's most high-tech cinema, the fourteen-screen **Tennispalatsi** at Salomonkatu 15. Cinema listings can be found at the kiosk outside the east entrance to Helsinki railway station and at the Finnkino (www.finnkino.fi) website.

Tennispalatsi

The Art Deco **Cinema Orion** (Eerikinkatu 15, tel: 02 9533 8131; https://kavi.fi) at the national audiovisual archive shows classic Finnish and foreign arthouse films.

BARS AND NIGHTCLUBS

Most of the city's nightlife is centred in the area around the Central Railway Station. The party tends to start late: it's common for people to have a few drinks at home before hitting the town from 11pm onwards. Bars can stay open until 2am, nightclubs until 4am. The official drinking age is eighteen and over but some clubs have a minimum age limit of 21 or 24. Entrance fees are anything from free to outrageous.

Designed by Alvar Aalto, the elegant **Ateljee Bar** (Yrjönkatu 26; tel: 0300 870 020; www.raflaamo.fi) on the fourteenth floor of the Sokos Torni Hotel is a fabulous place to sip a glass of champagne and contemplate the high life, with spectacular views that extend over the city and beyond.

After the auction houses and investment banks close for the day, their employees head to the opulent, chandeliered **Kämp Bar and Club** (Pohjoisesplanadi 29; www.hotelkamp.fi) for post-work cocktails and a wide selection of European wines. Another sophisticated choice is the basement **Goldfish** (Korkeavuorenkatu 21; tel: 010 323 2980; www.goldfish.fi), stylishly decorated and aptly located next to the Design Museum, it's notable for its world-class cocktails and exceptional champagne list.

The fringes of the Design District hold several small quirky bars that make for an interesting night. **Bar Llamas** (Iso Roobertinkatu 14; tel: 040 1809350) is an intimate reasonably priced Latin-themed cocktail bar, while the nearby Art-Decoesque **Bier-Bier** (Erottajankatu 11; tel: 04 4240 6326) unsurprisingly serves an epic selection of beers. **Liberty or Death** (Erottajankatu 5; http://sonofapunch.com), provides a darker Brooklyn vibe and

Elite

has better-than-average cocktails, and **The Riff**, just round the corner at Iso Roobertinkatu 3, is a good old-school Finnish rock'n'roll bar.

Base Bar (Kalevankatu 3 near Esplanadi; www.basebar.fi), is a real rock bar, unpretentious and down-to-earth, with a great atmosphere, bands at the weekend and known for its extensive and high quality choice of beers. So whether you're a die-hard rock enthusiast or simply seeking a place to unwind, this bar's energetic ambiance makes it a must-visit for those looking to experience Helsinki's vibrant nightlife scene.

For a laidback, international crowd, seek out the great Irish bar **Molly Malone's** (Kaisaniemenkatu 1C; tel: 020 719 1970; www.mollymalones.fi), just a few metres from the central train station, which comes to life each night with live music performances.

Several Helsinki bars are famous for their summer terraces, where people flock to enjoy the warm bright nights. One such place is the well-to-do **Elite** (Etläinen Hesperiankatu 22; tel: 09 6128 5200; www.elite.fi), filled with Art Deco flair. A few minutes' walk from the National Museum, this Helsinki institution was big amongst local artists back in its heyday. **Mattolaituri** (Yrjönkatu 24; tel: 04 4950 3225; www.mattolaituri.com), is a high-end restaurant with a seaside terrace, where you can enjoy beautiful sea views with a glass of champagne whilst relaxing on a sun lounger on their own private beach. At weekends, DJs provide tunes for the guests, and it changes from laid-back to party mode. A little distance from the city centre in the green surroundings of Kaivopuisto Park is the legendary summer restaurant **Kaivohuone** (Iso Puistotie 1, Kaivopuisto Park; open May–Aug; http://helsinginkaivohuone.fi), also a late-night party joint that attracts the young and beautiful.

Nightclubs often feature themed evenings and live music; for example the university-owned, rock-focused **Tavastia** (Urho Kekkosen katu 4–6; www.tavastiaklubi.fi); the six bars and three music areas that comprise the long-standing **Kaarle XII** (Kasarmikatu 40; www.kaarle.fi), which is the place to be on Thursday nights. Helsinki's vibrant nightlife truly has something for everyone, so you won't be disappointed.

THE LGBTQ+ SCENE

Helsinki is a tolerant, open city where LGBTQ+ visitors should feel at ease. Helsinki Pride (http://pride.fi) takes place over a week in late June, culminating in a parade that can attract over one hundred thousand participants.

As far as socialising goes, **Bar Loose** (Annankatu 21; www.bar loose.com) sells itself as "a liberal living room for good people", and is welcoming to all. An unmissable Finnish institution is **DTM** (Mannerheimintie 6 B; www.dtm.fi). "Don't Tell Mama", the largest gay bar/club in northern Europe, offers its patrons everything imaginable: from a daytime coffee bar to bingo to karaoke to a full-on nightclub with two dancefloors. Another upbeat club is **Hercules** (Pohjoinen Rautatiekatu 21; http://hercules.fi), which attracts a mostly male, over-thirties crowd.

SHOPPING

The main shopping district in Helsinki fits neatly into a rectangular area between the Central Railway Station, the Esplanadi, Mannerheimintie and Senate Square and the Market Hall. The two largest department stores and a shopping centre, connected by a tunnel, are to the east along Mannerheimintie, near the station.

Aleksanterinkatu and the smaller streets that cross it on a north–south axis contain some wonderful speciality shops: the "Tori Quarter", between Senate Square and Market Square, is full of design boutiques and chic cafés. The leading Finnish design brands have flagship stores on Esplanadi, as do many large international brands. East of the cathedral, the Kruununhaka district is good for antiques.

Iittala glassware

Design District Helsinki (www.designdistrict.fi) is a marketing concept used to publicise the city's art museums, galleries and cutting-edge designers. A handy map, available in the tourist office, shows the location of around one hundred boutiques selling clothing, jewellery and quintessentially Finnish homeware, located mainly in the Kamppi and Punavuori areas, a short walk southwest of the railway station.

The Finns have a flair for modernist design: the clean, functional lines that have influenced architecture and furniture throughout the world also turn up in locally made jewellery, clothing, glass and homeware. The Design Museum (see page 50) is a great place to bone up, with 75,000 Finnish-designed objects in its collection.

CERAMICS AND GLASSWARE

Iittala & Arabia Design Centre Store (Hämeentie 135; tel: 0204 3910; www.arabia.fi) is the largest outlet for Arabia ceramics, Iittala glass, and Hackman and Pentik homeware. It's about a 25 minutes' tram ride from downtown Helsinki, and often has discounted items. Sadly, the factory that used to be here has been converted into a mall, and most production is done in China these days.

CLOTHING AND TEXTILES

Joutsen (Museokatu 8 & Mikonkatu 1; tel: 020 749 5216; www.joutsen.com), the northernmost manufacturer of down products in the world, uses goose- and duck-down from the Arctic region to fill its toasty-warm products. These include everything from duvets and pillows to cosy slippers to an innovative range of coats and jackets. **Marimekko** (Pohjoisesplanadi 33; tel: 050 572 5632; www.marimekko.com) is the quintessential Finnish clothing designer, selling bold, brightly coloured items for men, women and children, as well as textiles for home use.

Samuji (Liisankatu 17; tel: 040 014 9360; www.samuji.com) offers simple, stylish women's and men's clothing lines, created by some of Finland's best independent designers, with clean lines and a strong minimalist influence.

DEPARTMENT STORES

Stockmann (Aleksanterinkatu 52B; tel: 091 211; www.stockmann.fi), dating back to 1862, is the king of department stores, a seven-floor, city-block-hogging, age-old institution. You'll find plenty of high-quality Finnish merchandise here, and an excellent souvenir department. The connected Academic Bookstore (Akateeminen Kirjakauppa), designed by Aalto, is spread over four floors.

Sokos (Mannerheimintie 9; tel: 010 766 5100; www.sokos.fi) is a smaller department store, based in an emblematic building that opened in 1952 for the Olympic Games.

FINNISH SPECIALITIES

Moomin Shop (Mannerheimintie 20 and at Helsinki-Vantaa Airport; tel: 040 192 0720; www.moominshop.fi), a small but perfectly stocked outlet on the 2nd floor of the Forum shopping centre, will be heaven on earth for fans of Moomintroll, Snufkin and Little My.

Sauna Boutique (Unioninkatu 32; tel: 0452243015; www.saunamarket.fi) is the place to stock up on all your sauna essentials, such as sauna hats, bathrobes, birch whisks, skin-care products and sauna snacks.

JEWELLERY

Kalevala Koru (Pohjoisesplanadi 25-7, and at the Airport Shop at Helsinki Airport; tel: 0207 611 390; www.kalevalashop.com) is a fascinating jewellery store created in 1925 and owned entirely by a 2500-strong women's association. The Kalevala range is inspired by the Finnish epic poem, with pieces rendered in gold, silver and bronze. The store also sells silver Lapponia jewellery, once worn by Princess Leia in *Star Wars*. Both jewellery lines make occasional use of spectrolite, an unusual mineral in iridescent shades of green, dark blue and yellow.

MARKETS AND FLEA MARKETS

Helsinki's markets are full of colour and atmosphere and definitely worth a browse. **Kauppatori**, near the south harbour, is the main Helsinki market, and offers some attractive souvenirs, dolls, and leather and fur items on its stalls. The nearby Old Market Hall has an exceptional selection of delicatessen foods including unusual delicacies like bear meat. If you're shopping in the "Design District", pop into **Hietalahti Market Hall** (hietalahden-kauppahalli.fi) for snacks or a sit-down meal. Outside in summer, the **Hietalahti Flea Market** sprawls across the market square. On one day in May and in August, the city has a **Cleaning Day** (**Siivouspäivä**), where everyone can bring unwanted goods out and sell them on the streets.

SHOPPING CENTRES

Forum (Mannerheimintie 20A; www.forum.fi) is the largest shopping centre in

The sauna is a national institution and a way of life

central Helsinki with 120 shops. The lower level contains a food hall and a choice of restaurants.

Kamppi (Urho Kekkosenkatu 1; https://www.kamppihelsinki.fi) contains over one hundred retail stores, restaurants and supermarkets, while the basement holds the city's long-distance bus terminal.

SPORTS & ACTIVITIES

SAUNAS

A vital part of Finnish culture is the ubiquitous **sauna**. Historically, the sauna was where women gave birth and bodies were laid out after death, and for most Finnish people the sauna experience is still a serious, sometimes spiritual, one. Saunas are usually segregated between the sexes. The natural wood-burning types are the most highly valued: the beautifully peaceful **Kulttuurisauna** (Wed–Sun 4pm–9pm; charge; www.kulttuurisauna.fi) in the Merihaka district is a new spin on this ancient tradition.

Today, most people have saunas in their homes, but older public saunas remain in three districts northeast of the city centre in the Kallio/Sörnäinen. Entry costs between €13 and €23. Towels may need to be rented, and snacks are available:

Kotiharjun (Tue–Sun 2pm–8pm; charge; www.kotiharjunsauna.fi), at Harjutorinkatu 1, is another wood-burning sauna, dating back to 1928.

Löyly Sauna (Mon 4–10pm, Tue–Thur 1–10pm, Fri–Sat 1–11pm, Sun 11am–9pm, morning sessions Tue and Sat 9–11am; charge; www.loylyhelsinki.fi), built in 2016 at Hernesaarenranta 4, is a stunning wood-clad venue that also has a restaurant with terrace overlooking the old harbour area.

Nuuksio National Park

Sauna Hermanni (Mon–Fri 3pm–8pm, Sat 2pm–6pm; charge; www.saunahermanni.fi), at Hämeentie 63, has a 1950s vibe.

Sompasauna (daily 24hr; free; www.sompasauna.fi), at Verkkosarenkuja 6, is a no-frills open-air public sauna located right next to the sea, and a memorable Finnish experience. The saunas are mixed, clothing-optional, and there are no showers or changing rooms, though lockers are available if you bring your own padlock.

NATIONAL PARKS

Roaming forests and fells is an extremely popular pastime all over the country, encouraged by the legal concept of everyman's right, which allows wide-ranging access to the countryside. Finland has 38 national parks, managed by Metsähallitus (Finnish Nature Centre Haltia at Nuuksiontie 84, in Espoo, tel: 0206 39 4000, http://www.nationalparks.fi). **Sipoonkorpi** and **Nuuksio** (see page 72) national parks are just 20km and 35km from Helsinki respectively,

Pihlajasaari Island

and easily accessed by public transport. Their visitor centres can provide further information about hiking, skiing, snow-shoe walking, trail running, canoeing, mushroom picking and guided nature walks.

Finland is also a fine place for **birdwatching**: many migratory birds stop here before their yearly mass migrations. For more information, visit Bird Life Finland (www.birdlife.fi).

WATER ACTIVITIES

The country's wiggling shoreline provides visitors with excellent paddling opportunities. Natura Viva (00 358 10 292 4030; http://naturaviva.fi) offers two-hour guided **sea kayaking** tours as well as overnight stays to allow for exploration into the Helsinki archipelago.

Hietaniemi Beach (known to locals as 'Hietsu') is Helsinki's biggest family beach, with a gently sloping swimming area manned by lifeguards between June and mid-August. Take bus 55A from Kamppi. In summer, Helsinki's citizens also flock to the recreational **Pihlajasaari Island**, with sandy beaches (including a naturist beach) and sauna. The island can be reached by ferry from Merisatama harbour between mid-May and August.

SPECTATOR SPORTS

The main spectator sport is **ice hockey**, a major Finnish passion. The season runs from September to April. IFK Helsinki plays home matches at the Helsinki Ice Hall (Helsingin Jäähalli), just north of the Olympic Stadium; while Jokerit have an uncertain future due to being Russian-owned, though it looks likely they will also play at the Helsinki Ice Hall.

ACTIVITIES FOR CHILDREN

Family attractions in Helsinki include the **Korkeasaari Zoo** (see page 68), **Linnanmäki Amusement Park** (see page 60), and a small aquarium, **Sea Life Helsinki** (tel: 09-565 8200; www. sealife.fi), with displays from the tropics to the Baltic and a walk-through underwater glass tunnel. On the third floor of the National Museum (see page 43), **Workshop Vintti** (Tue–Sun noon–4pm) is an interactive exploration of Finland's history – kids can build a log house, harness a horse, weave a rug and sit on an emperor's throne!

Just a fifteen-minute train ride from downtown Helsinki, **Heureka** (tel: 09 8579 288; www.heureka.fi), the Finnish Science Centre at Tiedepuisto 1 in Vantaa-Tikkurila, has a range of "hands-on" exhibitions, a planetarium and some bas-ketball-playing rats.

Serena Water Park (tel: 09-887 0550; www.serena. fi) in Espoo can easily be reached by bus from Helsinki and is open year-round.

Linnanmäki Amusement Park

WHAT'S ON

Early Jan: Lux Helsinki (www.luxhelsinki.fi) Art installations created using light illuminate the city.

Early Feb: Musica Nova (http://musicanova.fi) Week-long contemporary music festival, held in alternate odd years.

Mid Feb: Parade of Graduating Students along Esplanadi.

Good Friday: Via Crucis. Passion-play procession, from Kaisaniemi Park to Senate Square.

Easter Saturday: Easter Bonfires. Bonfires on Seurasaari Island scare away witches, who traditionally wreak havoc today.

April Jazz Espoo: (www.apriljazz.fi) Helsinki's largest jazz event, in Espoo.

1 May: May Day. Traditional parades and a huge picnic in Kaivopuisto Park.

Early May: Lovely Helsinki. The city is decorated with flowers to celebrate spring; Cirko Festival (www.cirko.fi/en).

Late May: World Village Festival (www.maailmakylassa.fi/english) Free family festival with a multicultural focus – music, dancing and food.

Mid-June: Taste of Helsinki four-day culinary festival, hopefully restarting again in 2024 after the pandemic (contact tourist office for latest).

12 June: Helsinki Day (www.helsinkipaiva.fi/en) Happy Birthday, Helsinki! Fun-filled celebration to mark the city's founding in 1550.

21 June: Midsummer's Eve. Traditional bonfires on Seurasaari Island.

End June: Tuska Open-Air Metal Festival (www.tuska-festival.fi) Biggest heavy-metal festival in Northern Europe, held at Suvilahti power plant.

Mid-August: Helsinki Festival (www.helsinkifestival.fi) Finland's biggest cultural festival is a two-week celebration packed with music, film, art and theatre.

Early September: Helsinki Design Week (www.helsinkidesignweek.com).

Early October: Helsinki Baltic Herring Fair. Fishermen sell herring and other archipelago products from their boats at Market Square.

December St Thomas Christmas Market. Christmas gifts and handicrafts in Esplanadi Park.

6 December: Finnish Independence Day celebrations.

31 December: New Year's Eve. Music, speeches and singing in Senate Square, plus a fabulous firework display.

FOOD AND DRINK

FOOD HISTORY

Unlike other parts of Europe, Finland never had a strong bourgeoisie with the wealth and leisure to develop rich culinary traditions. The country's food history is a tale of austerity. Finland's isolated rural economy and unforgiving climate, with short summers and long winters, meant that harvested food had to last for six or more months. Finns depended on dried, smoked and pickled meats and fish dishes that would keep for several seasons.

Luckily for visitors, the situation today is different. Modern menus have been heavily influenced by the New Nordic Kitchen movement, which arose in Denmark in 2004. The movement advocates using local, organic and sustainable products, and has seen the Nordic countries, including Finland, develop a fresh pride and enthusiasm for ingredients that are unique to the region. There is also a sense of playfulness, as old-style "grandmother's" recipes are revisited and revitalised to suit modern tastes.

Finland was fought over for centuries by its Swedish and Russian neighbours, and both countries have had a heavy influence on its cuisine. Stroganoff, hotpots,

Outdoor cafés are popular in summer

Fresh seafood toasts

squidgy black bread, blinis, sauerkraut and pasties such as the rice-stuffed *karjalanpiirakat* hail from Russia; while meatball dishes, hard cheeses, and a startling selection of pickled herring are some of Sweden's gifts. The Swedish *smörgåsbord* has also found its way to Finland, where it is known as *seisova pöytä*. A few Helsinki restaurants also have Sámi-influenced menus, showcasing Arctic specialities such as reindeer and bear.

WHERE TO EAT

Helsinki has a wide selection of eating places, ranging from five Michelin-starred restaurants (Grön at Albertinkatu 3; Finnjävel Salonki at Ainonkatu 3; Demo at Uudenmaankatu 9–11; Olo at Pohjoisesplanadi 5; Palace at Eteläranta 10) to streetside kiosks selling grilled food. Most of the city's restaurants produce food to a high standard and have menus that change with the seasons: look for crayfish in July, chanterelles in August, Baltic herring in September, and goose, moose and reindeer in the autumn hunting season. There are also an increasing number of restaurants serving cuisine from other cultures, with classy Japanese, Chinese, Lebanese, Indian and Latin American options available.

As in other Nordic countries, where long winter days make summer sunshine all the more precious, outdoor cafés and bars are popular in the warmer months. It's a rare pleasure to sit on a green terrace, savouring a light lunch and watching the crowds pass by. Cafés are also the place to participate in a vital Finnish ritual, the consumption of coffee and *pulla*, sweet buns flavoured with cardamom.

Foodies should visit the city's markets. In summer, stalls on the market squares overflow with seasonal fruit and veg. In wintertime, head inside: the indoor market halls can provide you with fresh fish, meat and game, as well as delicatessen-style nibbles.

The Slaughterhouse (Teurastamo), just north of Kalasatama Metro station in the Sörnäinen district northeast of the centre, has become a foodie paradise with several restaurants and distilleries, and an eclectic mix of live music and cultural events (teurastamo. com), especially during the summer.

FINNISH CUISINE

Fish

Fish has always been important in the Finnish diet – unsurprising, considering the country's myriad lakes and rivers and long, long coastline. Bream, burbot, perch and pike are traditional species,

---

TASTES FROM THE TREES

Finland's whispering forests have added extra flavour to the nation's food. Edible substances have been found in all three of the country's most common trees. Birch gives Xylitol, a sweetener very kind to teeth; spruce spring shoots are used to make sweet jam, a delicacy served with desserts; and pine is a good source of tar, extracted from the tree in traditional tar-burning pits. The light tar has a soothing aroma and is used in Finnish sweets and ice cream. Pine is also raw material for the Finnish-invented Benecol, a margarine-style spread that has been found to have cholesterol-lowering qualities.

and salmon are omnipresent. What isn't available locally can be readily imported from neighbouring countries such as Norway.

Smoked fish is a speciality, although it may also be grilled, glow-fired, steamed, or basted in the oven.

Salmon soup (*lohikeitto*) is another subtle delicacy: only a pinch of salt is added to the liquid, but the main taste comes from the fish. Each way of cooking salmon in Finland gives a distinctive experience, but *graavi lohi* (raw salmon marinated for a day in salt and herbs) is delicious. *Graavi* is the Finnish version of *sushi* – but instead of rice and seaweed, it is served with small potatoes and dill.

While Finnish salmon should not be missed, don't forget to try *siika* as well. This white fish has a more subtle taste, and is also best in the *graavi* variety, with potatoes and dill. Tiny vendace (*muikku*), sometimes served with garlic and cream, are an ever-popular Finnish snack: this unpretentious little fish has more taste than all tropical varieties combined. Lamprey, a strange, jawless fish found in the rivers of western Finland, is another fine experience of Finnish haute cuisine. It is nearly always charcoal-grilled and eaten whole.

Tinned reindeer meat

Meat and game

Much of Finland's tasty elk meat disappears into private freezers during the hunting season, but semi-domesticated reindeer is more common. The Lapland speciality is *poronkäristys* (reindeer casserole), served with mashed potatoes and cranberry (lingonberry). The best part of reindeer is fillet steak, but a real delicacy is smoked reindeer heart, with a cedar aroma and a subtle taste. You can find this latter dish on the menu at Juuri (see page 114). The best restaurants in Finland also serve game birds in season (late summer/autumn), with wild duck being most common.

Vegetarians

Even as recently as twenty years ago, vegetarians were met with bafflement. Today there are several restaurants in the city that serve only vegetarian, vegan and gluten-free fare. Most other Helsinki restaurants have at least one vegetarian option on the menu.

Sausage (*makkara*) is very popular in summer – best grilled with local mustard. It also appears in the traditional Finnish soul food dish *pyttipannu*, a hash of fried potato, sausage and onions, topped with fried eggs. Meatballs (*lihapullat*) are another sturdy staple deriving from Sweden.

Vegetables, fruit and grains

Rye bread (*ruisleipä*) is king in Finland and served at every meal. It has an amazing ability to resist spoiling: in Finland's agrarian past, farmhouses had an annual baking day, and the resulting rye bread was then eaten over the course of the year. Common forms include leavened crispbread (*näkkileipä*), dried into thin slices; and the stickier, harder *jälkiuunileipä*, delicious with cheese and cold milk.

Barley is a traditional staple, which some restaurants are reintroducing to replace rice and pasta (which are common in Finland too). Barley, oats, rye and rice are all used for porridges, typical breakfast items in Finnish homes.

Potatoes are available all year round, but their most delicious incarnation is as the tiny, nutty new potatoes that come into season in July.

Root vegetables and brassicas traditionally kept Finns going through the winter. Swede, turnip and cabbage are seldom considered "gourmet food", but some restaurants such as Restaurant Aino (see page 112) make a virtue of them in dishes such as beef and barley-filled cabbage rolls (*kaalikääryleet*), served with mashed potatoes and lingonberry jam.

One special element in Finnish cuisine is the abundance of wild berries, fungi and herbs, gathered from the forests. Blueberries and sweet, wild strawberries are readily available in July, the native sour cranberries (lingonberries) by September. Out of 2,000 varieties of Finnish fungi, around five hundred are edible – many varieties turn up in restaurants and on market stalls in August and September.

Sweet treats

Berries are often used to create juicy desserts, such as blueberry pie, tart-tasting lingonberry pie, strawberry cake and the delightfully named *lakkakakku* (cloudberry cake).

Stodgier fare includes doughnuts and cinnamon buns, usually eaten with morning coffee. For a love-it-or-hate-it snack, look out for salt liquorice in supermarkets.

Coffee lovers

Soldiers building the Suomenlinna Fortress were the first to bring coffee to the country. Today, Finns are the world's biggest coffee drinkers, consuming a staggering 12kg (26 lbs 6 oz) per person per year!

Speciality food

Finland is a large country, and all kinds of regional delicacies have evolved over the years. Many make their way to Helsinki: look out for Tampere's *mustam-akkara* ("black sausage"), which contains spices, barley and blood in real gut; delicious Karelian pasties, filled with buttery rice; the strange, "squeaky" cheese *leipäjuusto*, from the north-west coast, often eaten with yellow cloudberries; and bear meat and reindeer stew (*poronkäristys*) from Lapland.

Coffee is big business in Finland

Christmas food in Finland is very traditional, and still very much loved, in spite of being rather simple by today's standards. Little has changed on the festive menu over the past century: ham, salmon, casseroles and dried codfish always feature, and there are plenty of desserts, including ginger biscuits and the popular star-shaped plum tart, *joulutorttu*. At Easter, Finns consume *mämmi* (a malt-based pudding) and drink *sima* (mead), while *tippaleipä* pastries are the May Day speciality. Festival times apart, Finnish food varies both seasonally and geographically, making it an endless source of fascination and providing pleasant surprises for visitors to the country.

Mealtimes

Mealtimes are early compared to some European cities – usually 6.30am–10am for breakfast, 11am–1pm for lunch and 6.30–9pm for dinner. Inexpensive lunches (*lounas*) can be had at cafés (*kahvilat*). Note that restaurants may close on Sunday and/or Monday, and many shut completely for the month of July.

WHAT TO DRINK

Medium-strength beer is available at most cafés, and a full range of beverages is sold at fully licensed restaurants and bars. Restaurants serve beer from 9am and other alcoholic drinks from 11am, but stop serving them half an hour before they close. The basic measures are 4cl (1.3fl oz) for spirits, 8cl (2.7fl oz) for fortified wines and 12cl (4fl oz) for table wines; beer is served either in 0.33-litre (0.7 pint) bottles or in 0.4-litre (0.8 pint) glasses. Not all restaurants are licensed, so check before you go. The minimum legal age for drinking alcohol in restaurants is eighteen.

Beer is ubiquitous, and one of the "big five" is most usually served: Koff, Lapin Kulta, Karhu, Karjala or Olvi (this last is in fact the only major brewery still Finnish-owned). Most beer is usually 4.5 or 5.2 percent, stronger brews can reach seven percent.

The bar of The Helsinki Distilling Company

Wine is relatively expensive and often drunk with meals. You will find both local and imported vintages on offer. There are now around 25 wineries in Finland with strawberries, blackcurrants and redcurrants, among other local ingredients, used to produce a distinctive red wine –for those with an interest check out the Finnish Wineries website www.viinitilat.net.

Vodka is particularly popular in Finland and Finlandia is the country's best-selling brand, distilled with crystal-clear water that has been naturally filtered through deep moraine ridges. Berries grow everywhere and the Finns use them to make liqueurs, such as Lapponia Lakka, which is made from cloudberries.

The sale of alcohol is strictly controlled in Finland; strong beer (over 4.7 percent), spirits and wine can be bought only from Alko (the state alcohol monopoly); Stockmann's department store in Helsinki has an Alko unit on the ground floor. Medium- and lower-alcohol beer can be bought in supermarkets.

TO HELP YOU ORDER...

A table, please **Pöytä, kiitos.**
We would like to order... **Haluaisimme tilata...**
What do you recommend? **Mitä te suosittelette?**
Enjoy your meal! **Hyvää ruokahalua!**
Could I have the bill, please? **Saisko laskun, kiitos?**

Beer **olut**	meat **liha**
bread **leipä**	menu **ruokalista**
butter **voi**	milk **maito**
coffee **kahvi**	pepper **pippuri**
dessert **jälkiruoka**	potatoes **perunoita**
fish **kala**	rice **riisi**
fruit **hedelmät**	salad **salaatti**
ice cream **jäätelö**	salt **suola**

sandwich **voileipä**
soup **soppa**
sugar **sokeri**

tea **tee**
water **juomavesi**
wine **viini**

...AND READ THE MENU

ankerias eel
grillattua grilled
hampurilainen hamburger
hauki pike
hernekeitto pea soup
hirvenliha elk
juusto cheese
kakku cake
kalamurekepihvit fishcake
kana chicken
karjalan piirakka Karelian
   pasty
kinkku ham
kirjolohi rainbow trout
lammas lamb
lihapullat meatballs
lohi salmon
makkara salami
mansikka strawberry
mäti fish roe
merenelävät seafood
muikku vendace
muna egg
muurain arctic cloudberry
mustaherukka blackcurrant
nakki hotdog

naudanliha beef
omena apple
palapihvi beef casserole
perunoita potatoes
piimä buttermilk
pihvi steak
porkkana carrot
poronliha reindeer
pulla bun
puolukka lingonberry
puuro porridge
rautu arctic char
ruisleipä dark rye bread
savusilli smoked herring
sianliha pork
sieni mushroom
siiki whitefish
silakka Baltic herring
simpukka mussel
sinappi mustard
suklaa chocolate
turska cod
vaapukka raspberry
vasikanliha veal
vihannekset vegetables

WHERE TO EAT

We have used the following symbols to give an idea of the average cost of a three-course meal without wine:

€€€	over €60
€€	€35 to 60
€	below €35

RAUTATIENTORI

Food&Co. Pääposti € *Mannerheiminaukio 1B, tel: 020 729 6712,* www. compass-group.fi. This lunch restaurant, set in the main post office building next to the railway station, does a grand selection of traditional Finnish dishes, priced at a reasonable €10 (€2 extra for dessert). Note it's only open weekdays (till 2pm).

Napule € *Kaivokatu 8, tel: 09 640025,* napule.fi. Located just across the road from the railway station, this classic Neapolitan-style pizzeria with a bright, modern interior hits the spot with its authentic pizzas and a handful of other pasta dishes and risotto (€10-20).

Natura €€ *Iso Roobertinkatu 11, tel: 040 689 1111,* www.restaurantnatura. com. This central eatery serves up very good Scandinavian cuisine with a focus on Finnish game, vegetables and seafood, and has a Michelin green star for its sustainable dining and organic ingredients.

Venn €€ *Mikonkatu 4, tel: 010 76 64672,* www.raflaamo.fi/fi/helsinki/venn-helsinki. Cosy if dark, this cheerful, busy spot is a restaurant/bar right off Esplanadi. Great wines and cocktails as well as burgers and sharing plates to soak up the alcohol.

Vltava €€ *Elielinaukio 2, tel: 010 766 3650,* www.raflaamo.fi/fi/helsinki/vltava. Ideally situated just next to the railway station, this Czech restaurant serves thick *wursts* and traditional sausages. They're also renowned for their beer selection, culled straight from the best areas of the Czech Republic.

MARKET SQUARE AND ESPLANADI

Esplanad € *Pohjoisesplanadi 37, tel: 09 665 496,* www.esplanad.fi. This classic establishment doesn't have the best decor, but in terms of central city cafés, there isn't that much that can beat it for location. In addition to the great fresh-brewed coffee, there are sandwiches, soups and snacks. Best for coffee and cakes, consumed at a sunny outdoor seat.

FOC Tapas & Pintxos €€ *Unioninkatu 18, tel: 04 5801 4405*, www.foc tapas.com. A slice of Spain in Helsinki, the *tapas*, Spanish wines, ambience and service are exceptional at this recently opened family-run restaurant.

Haven €€€ *Eteläranta 16, tel: 09 6824 2840;* www.hotelhaven.fi. This restaurant, next to Market Square, is inside a nineteenth-century Empire-style building – the second oldest in the city - designed by Engel. The building and decor are traditional and the cuisine, although traditional, has a modern twist. A good place for brunch.

Kappeli €€ *Esplanadi Park, tel: 010 766 3880,* www.kappeli.fi. This classic, grand house – forged out of glass and iron – dates back to 1867. It looks right onto the Esplanadi and is perhaps the most popular place for people to come and unwind. Lots of live entertainment both inside and out during the summer. Classic Finnish dishes, from light open sandwiches to mains of reindeer and salmon.

Café Ursula €€ *Ehrenströmintie 3, tel: +358 965 281 7,* www.ursula.fi. Huge south-facing café with some of the best views of the water you'll find in the city. A little pricy, but worth it, and they do great ice-cream as well as Finnish/international set lunches, and à la carte for dinner.

KATAJANOKKA

Everest Katajanokka € *Luotsikatu 12A, tel: 050 471 7003,* dev.everest nokka.fi. A five-minute walk east of the Cathedral, this Nepalese restaurant is one of the oldest South Asian joints in town, and serves a mix of Nepalese and Indian dishes, including many vegetarian options. Some dishes come with their excellent *naan* bread included, and the set *thali* plates are superb.

Nokka €€€ *Kanavaranta 7 F, tel: 09 6128 5600,* nokkahelsinki.fi. Located in one of the old red-brick buildings under the Orthodox Cathedral, this is a restaurant of great character with exposed brick walls, wooden beams and an eclectic decor featuring, among other things, propellers and old divers' helmets as light fittings. The menu features plenty of wild fish, reindeer, partridge, and wild mushrooms, with wild berries for puddings. The five-dish tasting menu is highly recommended.

Shelter €€ *Kanavaranta 7, tel: 010 207 3002,* www.ravintolasipuli.fi. This comfortable and relaxed Scandinavian/European restaurant is set in the same restored warehouse as Nokka, and has two floors, as well as a summertime terrace. The small, rich gastro menu here changes quite often, but the steak tartar is the current favourite, and dishes (and chef's menus) can be paired with wines from its extensive list.

MANNERHEIMINTIE

Aino €€€ *Mannerheimintie 56, tel: 050 538 7690,* www.ravintolaaino.fi. The Aino has a fine location near the Finnish National Opera and a relaxing atmosphere. The menu of well-presented and contemporary Finnish dishes includes local fresh- and salt-water fish, lamb, reindeer, root vegetables, wild mushrooms and berries, with wine or beer pairings for each. Try and get a seat in the quieter and more pleasant courtyard dining area.

Ateljé Finne €€€ *Arkadiankatu 14, tel: 010 281 8242,* www.ateljefinne.fi. This intimate little spot was once the studio of sculptor Gunnar Finne, and it maintains an arty atmosphere and clientele. Traditional Finnish dishes are given a modern bistro twist – don't leave without trying the liquorice-spiced crème brûlée.

Farang €€€ *Ainonkatu 6, tel: 01 0322 9385,* http://farang.fi. Reputedly one of Helsinki's best Asian restaurants, this place infuses fresh ingredients with finely balanced flavours, although the new premises are somewhat cramped. Its fusion food is innovative without being pretentious – and veggies can delight in a tasting menu of their very own.

Kuu €€ *Töölönkatu 27, tel: 09 2709 0973,* www.ravintolakuu.fi. This relaxed bistro is handy for pre-opera dining – the Opera House is just 300m away. "The Moon" serves Finnish classics and related Scandinavian fare, such as smoked salmon soup, reindeer steaks and rhubarb pie.

Lasipalatsi €€ *Mannerheimintie 22–24, tel: 020 742 4290,* www.ravintola lasipalatsi.fi. Between the railway station and the bus station, this restaurant is located in the functionalist "Glass Palace" and has 1930s-style decor in keeping with the building. The menu, like the seasons, changes four times a year and features typical Finnish ingredients such as fresh fish, local cheeses and full-flavoured wild berries.

THE "DESIGN DISTRICT"

Café Bar No 9 €€ *Uudenmaankatu 9, tel: 09 621 4059,* http://bar9.net. A few minutes' walk away from the Swedish Theatre, at the head of the Esplanadi, this relaxed little café/bar is popular with a younger, student crowd. The single-page menu offers a surprisingly wide variety of sandwiches, salads, soups, stir-fried dishes and pasta, all at very economical prices.

Fuji Biyori € *Korkeavuorenkatu 47, tel: 04 0687 8073,* fujibiyori.com. Excellent Japanese fusion cuisine, served up in an unpretentious wood-panelled interior, the menu has influences from all over Japan and changes with the seasons. *Ramen*, *Sashimi* and *sake* are available all year, however, and the lunch sets are great value.

Magu €€ *Korkeavuorenkatu 27, tel: 04 4737 3355,* maguhelsinki.fi. This central restaurant with a traditional dining room serves well-presented and imaginative vegan fare that will impress even the most dedicated carnivores. Using locally produced seasonal ingredients, the ever-changing menu features wine pairings for each dish, two extensive tasting menus, and its ecological credentials are second-to-none. Choose Magu for a conscious dining experience.

Salve €€ *Hietalahdenranta 11, tel: 010 766 4280,* www.raflaamo.fi/fi/helsinki/salve. This historic and somewhat Bohemian restaurant-pub serves good traditional Finnish meals in a distinctly maritime atmosphere and is particularly famous for its fried herring (though drinking is often a more popular reason to come here). Looks onto Helsinki's world-famous shipyards.

ULLANLINNA AND KAIVOPUISTO

Saslik €€ *Neitsytpolku 12, tel: 09 7425 5500,* ravintolasaslik.fi. Rebranded as a Slavic rather than a Russian restaurant since the War in Ukraine, this longstanding Helsinki institution serves up high-end chicken Kiev, *Borscht* soup and even bear *stroganoff*, though it's most famous for its *blinis*. Slavic troubadours perform every Saturday night.

Seahorse €€ *Kapteeninkatu 11, tel: 09 628 169,* www.seahorse.fi. This restaurant has entertained such celebs as Dizzy Gillespie and Pablo Neruda. Surprisingly, the menu is good value, even for the not-so-famous, and features some tasty Finnish classics such as herring, traditional meatballs and Pike Mannerheim.

KALLIO

Meripaviljonki *Meripaviljonki, Säästöpankinranta 3, tel: 020 742 5320,* www.ravintolameripaviljonki.fi. There was a huge buzz surrounding this beautiful floating glass restaurant when it opened in 2015 near Hakaniemi Market. The menu focuses on fresh fish dishes. Beautiful sea views are a bonus.

Raiku € *Hämeentie 1, tel: 044 323 2515,* http://raiku.net. A stand-out lunch restaurant, this cheerful, orange-painted place inside Hakaniemi Market Hall does simple soups, salads and hot mains to the highest standards. Every item on the daily changing menu is made from scratch on the premises, and there is always a veggie option.

SUOMENLINNA FORTRESS

Suomenlinnan Panimo €€ *Rantakasarmi, Suomenlinna C 1, tel: 020 742 5307,* www.panimoravintola.fi; *open year-round*. This is the best of Suomenlinna's sit-down restaurants, serving fresh fish and traditional meaty Finnish dishes, such as fried trout with crayfish sauce and roasted reindeer. The restaurant has its own microbrewery, concocting seasonal ales, and has a lovely sunny garden in which to enjoy them. Located in the Jetty Barracks (Rantakasarmi) next to the HSL ferry harbour.

HELSINKI'S ISLANDS

NJK €€€ *Valkosaari, tel: 09 6128 6500,* www.ravintolanjk.fi; *open May–Sept.* Several of Helsinki's islands contain nothing more than a seasonal restaurant. Valkosaari contains the Yacht Club's NJK, based in a turn-of-the-century villa. Summon the spirit of the Nordic summer by hopping aboard the tiny ferry (from Valkosaari pier, near Olympic terminal) and dining on crab or crayfish, while admiring views over the water to Market Square. Ferry price (€8) included in restaurant bill.

TRAVEL ESSENTIALS

PRACTICAL INFORMATION

A

ACCOMMODATION

Hotels in Finland have a well-deserved reputation for cleanliness, a wide range of facilities, good service and comfortable, albeit rather small, rooms, regardless of their price category. Official hotel ratings are not used in Finland, but the vast majority of hotels would be considered to be in the three- or four-star class. They do tend to be expensive for the facilities provided, although if you are patient, there are bargains to be had. Discounts are often available at weekends and in summer, when hotels lose their business and conference trade.

Most Helsinki options are international (Hilton, Radisson) or Finnish chain hotels, comfortable but unremarkable. Finnish chains include Best Western Finland (tel: 0800-12010, www.bestwestern.fi), Cumulus (tel: 09-73352, www. cumulus.fi), Finlandia Hotels (tel: 09 684 1440, www.finlandiahotels.fi), the Palace Kämp group (tel: 020 770 4705, www.kampcollectionhotels.com/), Scandic Hotels (tel: +46 8 517 517 20, www.scandichotels.fi), Sokos Hotels (tel: 020 1234 600, www.sokoshotels.fi), and the budget Omena Hotels (tel: 0600 555 222, www.omenahotels.com), who keep costs low by not having reception staff.

Most Helsinki hotels are in the centre of town in an almost rectangular area between Central Railway Station in the north, Esplanadi in the south, Mannerheimintie to the west and Senate Square and Market Hall to the east. There are a couple of larger ones along Mannerheimintie, overlooking Töölönlahti Bay and near Hakaniemi Market.

For something more homey, Helsinki Bed and Breakfast (Vellamonkatu 12-14 B 32, tel: 050 584 9054; http://en.hbb.fi) can fix you up with a comfortable B&B room or private apartment.

The website Visit Helsinki (www.visithelsinki.fi) keeps an up-to-date list of accommodation options.

AIRPORTS

Finland's main international airport, **Helsinki-Vantaa Airport** (www.

helsinki-vantaa.fi), is a modern facility with an excellent range of services located about 20km (12 miles) north of Helsinki city centre. It is connected by I or P train every ten minutes, or fifteen minutes on a Sunday (daily 5.30am–2.20am; €4.10) to Helsinki Central Railway Station which takes 27 or 32 minutes respectively. Outside these times, the same route can be done hourly by local bus #600 (€4.10) but takes fifteen minutes longer. There is also a "shared" taxi stand at the airport. Expect to pay around €45-50 for a taxi to any destination in the city centre.

B

BICYCLE RENTAL

Bicycles are a practical and fun means of transport in Helsinki: the city has several hundred miles of well-maintained cycle paths. A good year-round hire shop is **Bicyclean Helsinki Katajanokka** (Luotsikatu 14; tel: 044 2915 331; May–Sept Mon noon–6pm, Tues–Sun 10am–6pm, Oct–Apr Mon noon–4pm, Tues–Sat 10am–4pm; www.bicycleanhelsinki.com). Prices start from €20 per day.

BUDGETING FOR YOUR TRIP

Flights to Finland vary according to departure airport, carrier and time of year, but you can expect to pay around €250 to €350 for a return London–Helsinki flight in July in economy class if booked a few weeks ahead – it will cost more if not.

Compared to other countries in Europe, Finland is expensive. A dorm bed in a youth hostel costs around €20-30, while a hotel room is likely to cost upwards of €120 per night.

Many lunch places offer a good-value meal deal costing around €10, which usually includes a main course, plus salad or soup, bread and coffee. Otherwise, dining out is expensive. A three-course meal without wine at a mid-level restaurant costs around €50. Alcohol in a restaurant is equally pricey, with a 0.33 litre glass of beer costing around €7, and a small glass of wine from €8 upwards. Many bars and restaurants have a "wardrobe" charge of around €3, which you'll have to pay whether you have a coat on or not. Groceries tend to be around the EU average. Museum entrance usually costs between €6 and €12.

Those on a budget can enjoy the city's unusual architecture, wandering streets such as the Art-Nouveau Luotsikatu, or visiting Kamppi Chapel of Silence or Helsinki Music Centre. Suomenlinna makes a cheap day trip – you can visit this extraordinary island for the price of a local-transport ticket (€5). Cheap places to eat include the coffee tents in Helsinki's market squares, while late at night you can find fairly inexpensive food (for example a €3 hamburger) at a *grilli* kiosk. Some museums offer free entry on a certain day of the month. Discounts for seniors and students are widely available.

C

CAMPING

Rastila Camping Helsinki (Karavaanikatu 4; tel: 09 310 78517; rastilacamping.hel.fi; open year-round) is a modern five-star campsite, with eighty tent and 165 caravan pitches, 21 cabins and cottages for hire, and a traditional barn that sleeps up to twenty. It's in Vuosaari, about 15km (9 miles) east of Helsinki centre and is easily accessed from the Rastila Metro station. Booking ahead is strongly advised in summer.

Finland has some 330 campsites. For options elsewhere in the country, see the website of the Finnish Camping site Association (Suomen Leirintäalueyhdistys; Tulppatie 14, FI-00880 Helsinki; tel: 09 4774 0740; www.camping.fi).

CAR HIRE

A car is not really necessary in Helsinki. The city centre is very walkable, and the public transport system is excellent.

If you do feel in need of a car, several international agencies have outlets at the airport, and also in the centre: Avis (Malminkatu 24; tel: 010 436 2222; www.avis.fi), Europcar (Mannerheimintie 56; tel: 0403 062 803; www.europcar.fi), Hertz (Runeberginkatu 5; tel: 020 555 2300; www.hertz.com), Sixt (Kampinkuja 1; tel: 020112 2550; http://fi.sixt.com).

CLIMATE

Helsinki is actually quite mild considering its latitude. Although the North Atlantic brings cold air, the moderating influence of the warming Gulf Stream keeps the temperatures bearable. The city has four seasons. Summers are generally pleasant and mild – the brightest month is June, with nineteen hours of sunlight, and the warmest is July, with an average temperature of 17.8°C (64.0°F). The air gets crisp and cold in September, as autumn approaches. Winters can be bitter: the coldest time is late January/early February, when temperatures can drop as low as –15°C (5°F) and the sea freezes over. After the chilly winter darkness, the coming of spring in April is a welcome relief.

CLOTHING

The weather in Helsinki is changeable – the best advice is to bring layers of clothing, regardless of the season. Finns tend to dress down, unless attending an important formal occasion. Generally, you won't feel out of place anywhere in casual clothing.

Finland can get very hot in summer. Sun block and a sun hat are a must, as is a swimsuit for the many sandy beaches around the city. However, you can't always depend on temperate weather. Bring a raincoat, just in case; and a fleece or similar to keep off the cool evening air. Many of the city streets are cobbled, so it's a good idea to wear sturdy walking shoes.

Helsinki is famous for its bitter winters, when decent cold-weather outer clothing is a must. Again, though, layers are key – most Finnish buildings are very well heated in winter, so you'll want to be able to peel off once you get inside. Don't forget to bring heavy-duty, warm footwear (preferably boots) with a good grip, as roads and pavements can be icy.

CRIME AND SAFETY

Finland is one of the safest countries in Europe, and for the most part crime will not be an issue. Occasional pickpocketing has been known on the Helsinki metro and at the main railway station. Be alert in crowded places or when using cash machines, take common-sense precautions with valuables and you will be fine.

The police in Finland generally keep a low profile. If you need to report a crime, the police station is at Pasilanraitio 13, tel: 0295 470 011 (Daily 8am–4.15pm).

D

DISABLED TRAVELLERS

Finland has good legislation in place for disabled people, and all new buildings are legally required to have access in terms of ramps, lifts, toilets, etc. Helsinki metro is accessible for wheelchair-users, but other forms of public transport may be a bit more problematic, although some city buses "kneel", making it easier to board, and many tram stops are raised. The state railway VR has induction loops and Braille numbering on newer trains. Assistance is available for wheelchair users by contacting VR barrier-free travel service (tel: 0800 188 822, www.vr.fi). Wheelchair spaces are limited, so it's best to reserve one ahead of time. When ordering a taxi, specify your needs.

wheelchair **pyörätuoli**
Is there..? **Onko siellä...?**
access for the disabled **esteetön pääsy liikuntaesteisille**
a wheelchair ramp **pyörätuoliluiska**
a disabled-accessible toilet **invalidi-WC**

DRIVING

Drive on the right, overtake on the left. Traffic approaching from the right has right of way. Exceptions are on roads marked by a triangle sign; if this is facing you, you must give right of way; similarly, if you are on a very major thoroughfare, it is likely that the feed-in streets will have triangles, giving you the right of way. On roundabouts, the first vehicle to reach the roundabout has right of way.

Speed limits are signposted. Generally, the limit in built-up areas is 30kmph (18mph); outside built-up areas, it is usually 80kmph (50mph) unless otherwise indicated; and on motorways 100kmph (62mph) to 120kmph (75mph). In winter, motorway speeds are generally 20kmph (12mph) lower.

Use of headlights is compulsory, even during the daytime (UK cars must sweep their lights right). Wearing of seat belts is also compulsory. A hands-free mobile must be used if you intend to use the phone while driving. Snow tyres are required December to February. Never ever risk driving while drunk in Finland. The limit is very low (0.5 percent blood alcohol) and the fines very steep; imprisonment is also not unheard of.

It is compulsory to carry a warning triangle, to be used in the event of a breakdown. Hazard warning lights should only be used if your vehicle is stranded in a place where it may cause danger to other vehicles.

Is this the way to…? **Meneekö tämä tie… -n/…-lle?**
Can you show me on the map? **Voitteko näyttää minulle kartalta?**
Can I park here? **Voinko pysäköidä tähän?**
My car broke down/won't start. **Autoni meni epäkuntoon/ei käynnisty.**

E

ELECTRICITY
Finland uses electricity at 220 volts AC (two-pin plug).

EMBASSIES AND CONSULATES
Australia: There is now an Australian consulate at Museokatu 25 B 23, tel: 010 420 4492, australian.consulate@tradimex.fi or the nearest embassy is in Stockholm (sweden.embassy.gov.au)
Canada: Pohjoisesplanadi 25B, tel: 09 228 530, www.canadainternational.gc.ca

Ireland: Erottajankatu 7A, tel: 09 682 4240, www.embassyofireland.fi
New Zealand: The nearest New Zealand embassy is in the Stockholm, Sweden, at Skarpögatan 6 tel: +46 8 400 17 270, www.mfat.govt.nz
South Africa: Nearest embassy is in Stockholm, Sweden at Alsnögatan 7, tel: +46 8 24 39 50, dirco1.azurewebsites.net/sweden
UK: Itäinen Puistotie 17, tel: 09 2286 5100, www.gov.uk/government/world/finland
USA: Itäinen Puistotie 14B, tel: 09 616 250, fi.usembassy.gov

EMERGENCIES

The all-purpose emergency number for police, fire, ambulance and rescue services is 112. There's also a 24-hour medical advice hotline, tel: 10 023.

G

GETTING THERE

Finnair (www.finnair.com) is the national carrier of Finland. In cooperation with British Airways, it operates daily flights between London and Helsinki, Manchester and Helsinki, and Edinburgh and Helsinki. Finnair also links with several North American cities including New York. You may be able to find value-for-money package fares and charter flights from New York or London, but they are rare; try the internet sites of the airlines for offers.

Budget airline Norwegian Air (www.norwegian.com) flies year-round between London Gatwick and Helsinki.

GUIDES AND TOURS

Tram Tours. Trams are omnipresent in Helsinki. Trams No. 2 and 3 traces a figure-of-eight course around the centre of Helsinki in roughly one hour, passing many of city's most interesting sights. The tourist office even provides a brochure, "Sightseeing on 2 and 3", for extra self-guided information.

Visitors may find the comforts offered by the **SpåraKOFF** (tel: 0300 870 020, www.raflaamo.fi/fi/helsinki/sparakoff) more attractive. This is a tram coach converted into a pub, and from its bar you can enjoy refreshments while taking a forty-minute tour of Helsinki's main sights. Running between mid-May and the end of August, the tours start at Railway Square (Tues–Sat at 2pm, 3pm, 5pm, 6pm, 7pm; also in July at 8pm), but you can hop on and off at any of the stops.

Bus Tours. Helsinki Hop On-Hop Off Bus, arranged by Stromma (www. stromma.fi), runs from May to September and departs from the Esplanadi Park/Fabianinkatu every thirty to forty minutes from 10am-4pm and costs €34. It provides sound effects and commentary in ten languages, taking in all the most important and interesting sights in Helsinki. For the rest of the year it's called the **Panorama Sightseeing Bus Tour** and runs just once a day, departing daily at 11am, taking 1 hour 45 minutes to complete the route.

Architecture Tours. The tourist office has a free *Jugend Helsinki* brochure and an *Architecture Map* for sale: armed with these two leaflets, you can be your own tour guide to Helsinki's architectural gems. The No. 4 tram also takes you past some interesting buildings, starting from Art-Nouveau-rich Kataja-nokka and ending in Munkkiniemi.

Architecture buffs should contact *Archtours* (tel: 041 313 4029, www.arch tours.com), a travel agency specialising in tailor-made architecture tours.

Wildlife and Adventure Tours. Natura Viva (tel: 010 292 4030; www.natura viva.fi) offers guided kayaking trips in the Helsinki archipelago.

If you're here in winter, **Taiga Times** (tel: 040 560 5305; taigatimes.com) can take you hiking around the frozen Helsinki archipelago, among other icy activities.

Both companies offer tours to Nuuksio National Park, just 40km (25 miles) from Helsinki.

H

HEALTH AND MEDICAL CARE

Finland is a very safe country with an excellent health service. Visitors from the EEA are covered for emergency medical treatment on presentation of a European Health Insurance Card (EHIC); take your passport along as well as

ID. There is usually a nominal charge for treatment: a visit to a public health centre will cost between €16 and €30, while an overnight hospital stay will cost around €35. Almost any *terveysasema* (public health centre) or *sairaala* (hospital) will treat you. Non-EEA visitors should arrange health insurance before travelling.

Some pharmacies (*Apteekki*) have late opening hours. In Helsinki, the Yliopiston Apteekki pharmacy at Mannerheimintie 96, tel. 0300 20 200, has 24-hour service. You can also get round-the-clock medical advice by phoning 09-10023.

Tap water is exceptionally clean and safe to drink.

I'm sick. **Olen sairas.**
I need an English-speaking doctor. **Tarvitsen lääkärin, joka puhuu englantia.**
It hurts here. **Tähän sattuu.**

I

INTERNET ACCESS

The city of Helsinki has a free Wi-Fi network with non-passworded hotspots around the city centre (e.g. Kluuvi and Kamppi shopping centres, the railway station, Esplanadi).

L

LANGUAGE

The official languages of Finland are Finnish and Swedish, spoken by 89 percent and 5 percent of the population respectively.

Most people speak almost perfect English, so you will have no language problems, but mastering a few basic words is always appreciated (see cover flap for Essential Expressions in Finnish).

LGBTQ+ TRAVELLERS

LGBTQ+ lifestyles are readily accepted in Helsinki, though somewhat less so in smaller communities outside the capital. Helsinki has a number of gay night-life venues. A good resource for gay-friendly bars, clubs, hotels, saunas etc. is the GayMap section of the Swedish lifestyle magazine *QX* (www.qx.se/gay map). The week-long Helsinki Pride (pride.fi) is Finland's largest LGBTQ+ event. It takes place at the end of June and attracts around one hundred thousand visitors. Seta (Pasilanraitio 5, 2nd floor, Helsinki; www.seta.fi) is an organisation that campaigns for LGBTQ+ equality.

M

MEDIA

Newspapers. The Finns are avid devourers of news and are third in the world for newspaper-readers. The best-selling papers are the Finnish *Helsingin Sa-nomat* and the tabloid *Ilta-Sanomat*. The largest Swedish-language paper is *Hufvudstadsbladet*.

English-language newspapers usually appear a day or two after UK pub-lication, and can be found in the Central Railway Station, the airport and at least two bookstores (Suomalainen Kirjakauppa at Aleksanterinkatu 15, and Akateeminen Kirjakauppa at Pohjoisesplanadi 39).

Television and Radio. The Finnish national broadcasting service *Yle* oper-ates four television channels, six national radio stations, and 25 regional radio stations. Short English-language news bulletins can be heard on *Yle Mondo* (97.5 FM in the Helsinki region) at 3.30pm (Mon to Fri) and 3.29pm (Sat and Sun), and also daily at 3.55pm on *YLE Radio 1* (87.9 FM in the Helsinki region). The BBC's World Service and other English-language television channels are usually available in hotels.

MONEY

The Finnish currency is the euro (€), which consists of 100 cents. Bank notes are in denominations of 5, 10, 20, 50, 100, 200 and 500, and there are 1, 2, 5, 10, 20 and 50 cent coins as well as €1 and €2 coins. One- and two-cent coins are not widely used: prices are usually rounded off to the nearest five.

It's generally easiest to use ATMs or pay with debit or credit cards as you would at home. If you need to exchange money, there are many currency exchange points in Helsinki:

Helsinki-Vantaa Airport: Change Group (tel 09 6940 258) have exchanges in arrival halls 2A (open daily 6am–9pm) but terrible rates and high commission mean they are best only used in an emergency.

Railway Station: Forex (tel: 09 417 1017; Mon–Fri 9am–7pm, Sat 10.30am–6pm) **Stockmann** department store also has a currency exchange (8th floor, Aleksanterinkatu 52B; open Mon–Fri 9am–9pm, Sat 9am–7pm, Sun 11–6pm)

O

OPENING TIMES

Banks are open Monday to Friday 9.15am–4.15pm.

Museums are usually closed on Mondays.

Shops are usually open Monday to Friday 9am–5pm, Saturday 9am–3pm. Some of the bigger department stores and supermarkets stay open until 9pm Monday to Friday and until 6pm on Saturday. Most stores are closed on Sunday, except for those under the Helsinki Railway Station, some in the Forum shopping mall and some on the Esplanadi.

P

POLICE

Helsinki Police Department is located at Pasilanraitio 1, tel: 0295 470 011. Its lost-and-found department is open Mon–Fri 9am–1pm.

The emergency-only number for police, fire, ambulance and rescue services is 112.

POST OFFICES

The main post office is at Elielinaukio 2F (tel: 0200 71000; open Mon–Fri 8am–8pm, Sat–Sun 10am–2pm).

Mailboxes for second-class post are bright orange and widely available. Mailboxes for first-class post are bright blue and less commonly found.

PUBLIC HOLIDAYS

Fixed dates:

1 January *Uudenvuoden päivä* New Year's Day
6 January *Loppiainen* Twelfth Day
1 May *Vapunpäivä* May Day
6 December *Itsenäisyyspäivä* Independence Day
24 December *Jouluaatto* Christmas Eve
25 December *Joulupäivä* Christmas Day
26 December *Tapaninpäiv* Boxing Day

Moveable dates:

Late March/April *Pitkäperjantai* Good Friday
Late March/April *Pääsiäinen* Easter
Late May *Helatorstai* Ascension Day
End May/June *Helluntai* Whitsun
Late June *Juhannus* Midsummer's Day
Early November *Pyhäinpäivä* All Saints' Day

R

RELIGION

The Lutheran Church is the state Church of Finland, with 72 percent of Finns counted as Lutherans. There is a small Greek Orthodox population, and just two Catholic churches in Finland.

In Helsinki, services in English are held at the Rock Church on Lutherinkatu (see page 44); there are both Lutheran and ecumenical services here. There is also one synagogue and one mosque in Helsinki, for those of Jewish or Muslim faith.

As in all places of worship, visitors are expected to dress modestly and behave appropriately, adhering to a mutual respect for different religions and communities.

T

TELEPHONES

Calls to Finland: Dial the international code (00 in Europe, 011 in the US and Canada), then the country code (358), then the town or city area code *without* the initial zero, then the number of the person you are contacting.

Town/city codes: Helsinki 09; Porvoo 019; Tampere 03; Turku 02. To call Tallinn, Estonia, dial the country code 372 before the telephone number.

Calls in Finland: Dial the town/city code and the number of the person you are contacting. For directory enquiries, dial 020202. For overseas call assistance, dial 020208. For information on mobile phones, dial 9800-7000. The few remaining public phone boxes are all card operated. Hotels usually add surcharges for telephone calls made from your room.

Calls abroad from Finland: Dial 00, then the country code and number, omitting any initial 0 (for example, 00-44 for the UK; 00-1 for US numbers).

Mobile phones: The country is covered by the 900/1800 Mhz GSM network. Most European phones are compatible, although your phone must be unlocked in order to link up with the network. US phones work on a slightly different frequency, so US visitors should check with their phone company first regarding usability. As of 2017, inter-EU roaming charges have been abolished but if you live in the UK, you may or may not be charged extra for using your data allowance in Finland as a result of Brexit, so check with your phone company.

SIM cards: The cheapest way to make calls while in Finland is to buy a prepaid Finnish SIM card and use that in your own mobile phone. For around €10 you can get a SIM card with a Finnish number and €7-worth of talk time. The cards (and refills) can be picked up at any R-Kioski shop. You can also buy prepaid micro-SIM cards that can be used in devices such as iPads.

TIME ZONES

Finland is two hours ahead of Greenwich Mean Time (GMT), and seven hours ahead of Eastern Standard Time (USA).

TIPPING

Tipping is not common in Finland. Service charges are included in hotel rates, and in restaurant and taxi prices, so tips are not expected. However, if you have had particularly good service, a tip never goes amiss!

TOILETS

There are a few dozen automated public toilets throughout Helsinki which cost 50 cents to use: for example, near the Old Market Hall and in Esplanadi.

Men's (*Miehet*) and women's (*Naiset*) toilets are usually distinguished by symbols.

TOURIST INFORMATION

The very helpful and newly-opened **Tourist Information Office** (Aleksanterinkatu 24, tel: 09 3101 3300, open mid-May–mid-Sept Mon–Sat 9am–5.30pm, Sun 9am–4pm; mid-Sept–mid-May Mon–Fri 9.30am–5pm, Sat–Sun 9am–4pm; www.visithelsinki.fi) will provide you with all the maps, brochures and information that you need to explore the city. There's a smaller branch in the pavilion on Lyypekinlaituri, next to the Old Market Hall (open June–Sept daily 9am–4.15pm, and green-clad **Helsinki Helper** tourist guides roam the city-centre streets and cruise-ship harbours during summer months searching for lost-looking visitors.

You'll find more general information on Finland as a whole from the Finnish Tourist Board's website **Visit Finland** (www.visitfinland.com).

Helsinki Card. The **Helsinki Card** allows free admission to almost fifty museums and attractions, free travel on public transport in Helsinki (just beep your Helsinki card on the card reader), free travel on the ferry/waterbus to Suomenlinna and Korkeasaari, a free, guided city bus or boat tour, a guide book with maps in five languages, and discounts in some stores and restaurants. It can be purchased online at www.helsinkicard.com, or in person from the tourist office and kiosks and from most hotels. It costs €48 for one day, €58 for two days and €66 for three days, with prices for children (aged 7–16) being €24, €29 and €33 respectively (2023 rates).

Other Tourist Offices:

Fiskars Info is at Fiskarsintie 9, tel: 020 439 2099, www.fiskarsvillage.fi. Community-run information is available year-round Mon–Fri 8am–4pm.

Porvoo City Tourist Office is at Rihkamatori B, Porvoo, tel: 020 692 250, www.porvoo.fi. The office is open Mon–Fri 9am–3pm.

Tampere Tourist Office is only available via e-mail, telephone and web chat, tel: 03 5656 6800, www.visittampere.fi. It is available Mon–Fri 10am–4pm.

Turku Tourist Office is at Aurakatu 8, Turku tel: 02 262 7444, www.visitturku.fi. It is open Apr–Sept Mon–Thur 9am–6pm, Sat 9am–3pm; Oct–Mar closed Sat.

Tallinn Tourist Information Centre is at Niguliste 2/Kullassepa 4, Tallin tel: +372 645 7777, www.tourism.tallinn.ee. It is open June–Aug daily 9am–6pm, Sept, Apr–May Mon–Fri 9am–6pm, Sat–Sun 9am–4pm, Jan–Mar, Oct 9am–5pm, Sat–Sun 9am–3pm.

TRANSPORT

Taxis. All taxis have a yellow *Taksi/Taxi* sign, which, when illuminated, indicates the taxi is vacant. Taxis can be hailed in the street, or there are numerous taxi stands, for instance at Central Railway Station, Senate Square, Esplanade Park and the ferry terminals. To pre-book a taxi, dial 0100 0700. The cost of an advance order is €7.30 and this will be added to the fare shown on the meter. The basic day rate (2023 rates) is €5.50-7.70 depending on day and time, with the increments per kilometre or minute (from €1.20), depending on the number of passengers. There is an extra charge of €3.10 for large items of baggage and usually a minimum fee of €12-14. **Uber** operates in the Greater Helsinki region, Turku and Tampere, and are considerably cheaper.

Trams, Buses and Metro. Helsinki's efficient, integrated public transport system is operated by **Helsinki City Transport (HSL)**, www.hsl.fi. Tickets are charged according to a zoning system (A, B, C, D) so you'll need to check a zone map before purchase. The HSL area consists of Helsinki, Espoo, Vantaa, Kauniainen, Siuntio, Kirkkonummi, Sipoo, Kerava and Tuusula but most of Helsinki is zone AB. Single tickets and day tickets can be purchased using the HSL mobile app or from HSL ticket machines, R-kiosks and many other sales points throughout the city. Tickets cannot be purchased from bus or tram drivers.

Single tickets are ideal for occasional journeys, are valid for 80–110 minutes, and allow you to transfer between modes of transport within their validity. An AB single costs €3.10 and is valid for eighty minutes. Day tickets for zone AB, valid on trams, buses and the metro, costs €9/13.50/18/22.50/27/31.50/36 for one/two/three/four/five/six/seven days. All forms of transport are free for holders of the Helsinki Card (see page 131). Most buses and trams run from around 6am until 1am.

The metro system mainly serves to take commuters to and from the suburbs. Trams, especially No. 3, are much more convenient for seeing Helsinki's sights.

V

VISA AND ENTRY REQUIREMENTS

Passports and Visas. Citizens belonging to Schengen member states can enter Finland simply with a valid ID card. Most other Western countries, including Ireland, the UK, the US, Canada, Australia and New Zealand, do not need visas to travel to Finland – a passport will suffice, as long as it has been issued within the last ten years and will remain valid for three months after leaving Finland. Citizens of South Africa do need to obtain a Schengen visa before travel from the Embassy of Finland in Pretoria (330 Victoria Street, Waterkloof, Pretoria 0001, Republic of South Africa, tel: +27 12 343 0275; www.finland.org.za), and must also have a valid passport, as above.

If you are in any doubt, check the visa requirements on the website of the Ministry for Foreign Affairs in Finland (Ulkoasiainministeriö; http://formin.finland.fi).

Y

YOUTH HOSTELS

Hostelling International Finland (Suomen Retkeilymajajärjestö, SRM; Yrjönkatu 38B 15, 2nd Flr, 00100 Helsinki, tel: 09 565 7150, www.hostellit.fi) oversees three hotels in Helsinki. These are:

Eurohostel (Linnankatu 9, tel: 09 622 0470; www.eurohostel.fi) Next to the Katajanokka ferry terminal with 135 beds. Facilities include launderettes, sauna and café.

Both Helsinki Hietaniemenkatu 14, tel: 09 1311 4334; bothxhome.fi) Summer-only hostel with 326 small, modern single and twin rooms with their own shower and kitchenette. Residential but central location, book well ahead.

Hostel Suomenlinna (Suomenlinna C 9, tel: 09 684 7471; www.hostel helsinki.fi) In a stunning location within the Suomenlinna Fortress. Sleeps forty in dorms and offers three private rooms.

WHERE TO STAY

Hotels in Helsinki are a homogenous bunch of comfortable, unremarkable chain hotels. Most of them lie within a broad stripe sweeping from Senate Square west to the end of Bulevardi. A further handful are dotted here and there off Mannerheimintie, and the quiet residential Katajanokka district holds another clutch. Another couple lie behind the cathedral and near Hakaniemi Market. Most hotels are within easy walking distance, or at the very most a fifteen-minute bus- or tram-ride, from the city centre.

Helsinki is so small that there is no special benefit to staying in one area or another, apart from personal preference. Would you like your surroundings to be Neoclassical or Jugendstil? Would you prefer a sea view or one of Töölönlahti Bay?

Hotels are listed below first by area, in the order covered in the Where to Go chapter, and then alphabetically.

Approximate prices for a double room in high season:

€€€€	**Over €250**
€€€	**€150–250**
€€	**€75–150**
€	**Under €75**

RAUTATIENTORI

Grand Hansa Hotel €€€ *Mannerheimintie 5, tel: 029 320 0200;* www.prime hotels.fi . This is one of Helsinki's most emblematic hotels. Opened in 1833 as the *Hotel Seurahuone*, it was moved to its present position opposite the Central Railway Station in 1914. In 2023, it was sympathetically renovated, expanded, and rebranded under new management. There are now 219 very modern rooms and five suites, as well as a bistro, bar saunas and other high-end facilities.

Holiday Inn Helsinki City Centre €€ *Elielinaukio 5, tel: 0300 308 482;* www.ihg.com. Courteous staff and its central location make this large hotel a very convenient choice. Rooms are clean and well-priced, and although some overlook the bus station, excellent soundproofing means you don't hear a thing. Kids stay and eat free, and facilities include air-conditioning, a restaurant, lobby bar, mini-gym and a sauna.

Radisson Blu Plaza Hotel €€€ *Mikonkatu 23, tel: 020 1234 703;* www.radisson blu.com. Next to Central Railway Station and the Finnish National Theatre, this hotel occupies a building dating from 1917 that has been renovated to include up-to-date facilities. The 302 air-conditioned rooms include six suites and six rooms with disabled access and facilities. Prices are roughly ten percent lower when booked without breakfast.

MARKET SQUARE AND ESPLANADI

Fabian €€€ *Fabianinkatu 7, tel: 09 6128 2000;* www.hotelfabian.fi. The Fabian's slogan is "We don't mind if you stay longer" – and you certainly won't mind either with decent discounts on stays over seven days. The 58-room boutique hotel is one of Helsinki's best and brightest, with chic rooms full of clever design details. Its Lux rooms are designed for longer stays and come with kitchenettes. Conveniently located, two blocks away from the Old Market Hall.

Haven €€€ *Unioninkatu 17, tel: 09 681 930,* www.hotelhaven.fi. Helsinki's design hotel changed the face of luxury accommodation in the city when it opened in 2009. It's a refined option right at the harbourside, with a leather-outfitted lobby, a lovely bar, a fireplace and a library of leather-bound books. Rooms offers fantastic views of the Uspenski Cathedral and are equipped with Egyptian cotton linens and Byredo bath products. The better-than-average restaurant offers a wide range of cuisines and excellent breakfasts to set you up for a day of exploring.

Hobo Helsinki (GLO Hotel) €€ *Kluuvikatu 4, tel: 010 344 4400;* hobohotel.fi. This unique boutique hotel right off Alexanterinkatu features sizeable rooms which are set to open in 2024 and decorated in their famous contemporary and quirky style. Its services are what this chain is really known for – this branch will have an event space, weekend club and pop-up spaces for artistic collaboration.

Kämp Hotel €€€€ *Pohjoisesplanadi 29, tel: 09 576 111;* www.hotelkamp.com. Opened in 1887, this central Neoclassical five-star boasts 189 Belle Epoque rooms and suites with marble bathrooms, polished stonework and lavish furnishings that all evoke a very decadent glamour. There is a gourmet restaurant, a comfortable, relaxing bar and even a ballroom.

KATAJANOKKA

Eurohostel € *Linnankatu 9, tel: 09 622 0470;* www.eurohostel.fi. Next to the Katajanokka ferry terminal, this no-frills hostel has 135 rooms with shared facilities, as well as launderettes, sauna and café. Convenient for those travelling by ship, and just ten minutes' walk from the centre.

Katajanokka €€€ *Merikasarminkatu 1A, tel: 02 9320 0620;* www.hotel katajanokka.fi. Best Western Premier hotel is a fabulous choice with a unique history, being the only Helsinki hotel set in a former prison. The nineteenth century layout is preserved, and the well-soundproofed rooms are done up in designer furnishings and linens. Tram No. 4 runs here from the city centre, a journey of about ten minutes – get off at the Vyökatu stop.

Scandic Grand Marina €€€ *Katajanokanlaituri 7, tel: 09 16 661;* www.scandic hotels.com. Designed in 1911 by noted Finnish architect Lars Sonck, this Katajanokka hotel offers 470 exquisitely decorated and well-equipped rooms, plus extensive conference facilities, numerous restaurants, a heated garage and the SkyWheel Helsinki, revolves slowly outside.

KAMPPI

Both Heelsinki € *Hietaniemenkatu 14, tel: 09-1311 4334;* bothxhome.fi. This summer-only hostel has 326 small, modern single and twin rooms with their own shower, plus a kitchenette and fridge. Family rooms with extra beds and monthly rentals are also possible. The hostel is on a peaceful residential street. Short stays most easily booked (well ahead) through www.hotelsin-finland.net.

Finn €€€ *Kalevankatu 3 B, tel: 09 684 4360;* www.hotellifinn.fi. This is one of the city's smallest hotels, with just 35 rooms. Its central location and low prices make it a good budget choice, with small last minute discounts and promo codes available from the hotel website – twins are less expensive than doubles. Rooms are small, but clean and functional. No restaurant.

Helka Hotel €€€ *Pohjoinen Rautatiekatu 23, tel: 09 613 580;* www.helka.fi. A medium-sized independent hotel, within easy walking distance of the Central Railway Station. Helka has 150 rooms, all of which are decorated in a spare, modern Scandinavian style, with furniture designed by Alvar Aalto, and giant photos mostly of Finnish nature stuck to the ceiling! The complementary buffet breakfast is a stand-out affair.

Omena Hotelli €€ *Yrjönkatu 30 and Lönnrotinkatu 13, tel: 0600 555 222 (€9 booking fee when you make a phone reservation);* www.omenahotels.com/en. These two central Omena hotels are good for thrifty groups or families. Prices are per room, each one furnished with a double bed and two fold-out singles (€10 extra each), plus kitchenettes containing a microwave, kettle, coffee machine and fridge. Decor is simple but pleasant, with deep, dark woods. The chain saves on costs by avoiding reception staff: entry is by code, which you are given upon booking. Yrjönkatu is behind the Forum shopping centre, while Lönnrotinkatu is a few streets away by the Old Church.

Radisson Blu Royal €€€ *Runeberginkatu 2, tel: 020 123 4701;* www.radissonblu.com. Modern rooms with very comfy beds and sunny open dining and bar areas. A favourite with business travellers, and its location next to the Kamppi complex makes it handy for shopping, restaurants and nightclubs.

Scandic Hotel Simonkenttä €€€ *Simonkatu 9, tel: 0300 308 402;* www.scandichotels.com. This is a large, elegant hotel with modern architecture and ecological design. It's right by the bus station so consider getting a room on the 4th floor or above to lessen street noise – and, of course, to enjoy fine views over the city centre. The restaurant serves international and Scandinavian cuisine, and there's a roof-top pavilion, as well as a good sauna and gymnasium.

Sokos Hotel Torni €€€ *Yrjönkatu 26, tel: 020 1234 604;* www.sokoshotels.fi. Helsinki's tallest building, with thirteen floors, opened in 1931 and has rooms in both its Art Deco and Jugendstil buildings – try for those overlooking

the courtyard. Its restaurants and bars include the Ateljee (see page 113), with its panoramic views, the American Bar that specialises in cocktails, and O'Malley's, the city's oldest Irish bar. There are also four saunas.

MANNERHEIMINTIE

Helsinki Apartment €€ *Töölöntorinkatu 7, tel: 050 367 6916; www.helsinki apartments.fi.* These comfortable and stylish apartments offer an excellent alternative to anonymous Helsinki hotel rooms. The bright rooms contain classic Scandinavian furniture and have kitchens/kitchenettes and access to laundry facilities. The fourteen apartments, located around Kamppi and Töölöntori, have one- to four-bedrooms, and note that keys must be collected before 10pm.

Scandic Park €€ *Mannerheimintie 46, tel: 030 030 8407; www.scandichotels. com.* Directly across from Hesperia Park, this is a five-star affair. Economy and standard rooms keep things simple, with wooden floors and soothing colour schemes; superior rooms overlook the bay and are tremendously peaceful. The hotel has a top floor swimming pool and a swishy hot tub.

THE "DESIGN DISTRICT"

Anna €€€ *Annankatu 1, tel: 09-616 621; www.hotelanna.com.* This quiet, decently-priced hotel, with 64 comfortable, fairly homely rooms, is set in a shopping quarter in the city centre. A good place for people travelling alone – almost half the rooms are singles (**€€**).

Holiday Inn Hotel Indigo €€ *Bulevardi 26, tel: 09 4784 0000; www.ihg.com.* Award-winning Indigo has 120 boutique rooms, exuding chic Scandi-style. Some of its public areas have had input from up-and-coming Helsinki fashion designer Satu Maaranen. Facilities include a Body, Mind & Soul studio, a fitness centre and a yoga trapeze. The hotel also has an environmental focus including charging points for electric cars, has excellent facilities for the disabled, and is also pet-friendly.

Hostel Diana Park Erottajanpuisto € *Uudenmaankatu 9, tel: 050 338 5434; www.dianapark.fi.* This dinky HI (Hostelling International) hostel has a warm, welcoming atmosphere and cosy rooms, whether you choose a four- to six-bed dormitory or a private double. Most bathrooms are shared. It's deservedly popular, so book ahead. A ten-minute walk from the railway station; trams 3B and 6 run close by. Dorms €45.

Klaus K €€€ *Bulevardi 2-4, tel: 020 770 4701; www.klauskhotel.com.* Top-of-the-class Klaus K is a chic, family-run boutique hotel. Its small but gorgeous rooms are decorated with a Kalevala-inspired theme and come with every amenity. They're a breath of fresh air amongst Helsinki's often rather bland hotel options. The Sky Lofts have access to a rooftop terrace.

Radisson Blu Seaside Hotel €€€ *Ruoholahdenranta 3, tel: 020 1234 707; www.radissonblu.com.* Near the bottom of Bulevardi and Hietalahti Market, the Radisson has pleasing views over the western harbour and offers 349 modern, comfortable rooms. It's about 2.5km (1.5 miles) from the railway station – trams Nos. 7 and 9 stop almost outside. A good option if you're catching an early ferry to Tallinn.

Rivoli Jardin €€€ *Kasarmikatu 40, tel: 09 681 500; www.rivoli.fi.* In a town-house right in the heart of the business and shopping area, this 55-room hotel is quiet, clean and has a faintly old-fashioned feel. Rooms have been renovated, and are tastefully furnished with updated amenities; a buffet breakfast is included.

KALLIO

Hilton Helsinki Strand €€€ *John Stenbergin ranta 4, tel: 0300 308 488;* www.helsinki-strand.hilton.com. Just across the Pitkäsilta Bridge from the Botanic Gardens, the Hilton features an impressive atrium with glass lifts that show off the impressive waterfront view. Service is exemplary, and there is an indoor swimming pool.

Scandic Paasi €€€. *Paasivuorenkatu 5 B, tel: 09 2311 700,* www.scandichotels.fi. Close to Hakaniemi Market, and overlooking Eläintarhanlahti Bay, this hotel is packed with personality. Room decor is inspired by the area's colourful history, and there is a library and bicycle-borrowing scheme for guests. As well as a cosy library, there's also a panoramic floating restaurant.

SUOMENLINNA

Hostel Suomenlinna € *Suomenlinna C 9, tel: 09 684 7471;* www.hostel helsinki.fi. The hostel itself is pleasant but basic; but as it's the only place to stay within Suomenlinna Fortress, it's worth staying here for the novelty factor alone – you get to enjoy this Unesco World Heritage site when all the other tourists have taken the fifteen-minute ferry ride back to the city centre. Sleeps 39 in dorms with eight private rooms.

FURTHER AFIELD

Hilton Helsinki Kalastajatorppa €€ *Kalastajatorpantie 1, tel: 09 45 811;* www.hilton.com. This well-known business hotel has 238 comfortable rooms, each with a view of the sea or the verdant park around it. The hotel has its own private beach where you can stay in a deluxe glass IGLUX room, and has six tennis courts. It's out of the city centre, close to Akseli Gallén-Kallela's house Tarvaspää.

INDEX

THE **MINI** ROUGH GUIDE TO
HELSINKI

First Edition 2024

Editor: Lizzie Horrocks
Updater: Charles Young
Author: Fran Parnell
Picture Editor: Tom Smyth
Cartography Update: Carte
Layout: Grzegorz Madejak
Head of DTP and Pre-Press: Rebeka Davies
Head of Publishing: Sarah Clark
Photography Credits: Ari Karttunen/EMMA 73;
Bigstock 42; Governing Body of Suomenlinna/
Dorit Salutskij 66; Gregory Wrona/Apa
Publications 6T, 34, 37, 92, 101, 104; Helsinki
Tourism 12, 24, 28, 84, 87; Helsinki Zoo/Mari
Lehmonen 70; iStock 4TL, 4ML, 5T, 5M, 5M, 5T, 7T,
22, 26, 32, 83; Library of Congress 18; Marketta
Stenroth/Visit Helsinki 65; Micah Sarut/Apa
Publications 79, 80, 82; Public domain 5M, 14, 17,
21; Shutterstock 1, 4ML, 5T, 30, 49; Visit Finalnd
74, 76, 78; Visit Helsinki 5M, 6B, 7B, 36, 39, 41, 44,
46, 51, 52, 53, 54, 56, 59, 60, 62, 69, 88, 90, 95,
97, 98, 99, 107, 108; VisitFinalnd/Juho Kuva 11;
VisitFinland 102
Cover Credits: Uspenski Cathedral **Shutterstock**

Distribution

UK, Ireland and Europe: Apa Publications (UK)
Ltd; sales@roughguides.com
United States and Canada: Ingram Publisher
Services; ips@ingramcontent.com
Australia and New Zealand: Booktopia;
retailer@booktopia.com.au
Worldwide: Apa Publications (UK) Ltd;
sales@roughguides.com

Special Sales, Content Licensing and CoPublishing

Rough Guides can be purchased in bulk
quantities at discounted prices. We can create
special editions, personalised jackets and
corporate imprints tailored to your needs.
sales@roughguides.com; http://roughguides.com

Printed in Czech Republic

This book was produced using **Typefi** automated
publishing software.

Contact us

Every effort has been made to provide
accurate information in this publication, but
changes are inevitable. The publisher cannot
be held responsible for any resulting loss,
inconvenience or injury sustained by any
traveller as a result of information or advice
contained in the guide. We would appreciate
it if readers would call our attention to
any errors or outdated information, or if
you feel we've left something out. Please
send your comments with the subject line
"Rough Guide Mini Helsinki Update" to
mail@uk.roughguides.com.